D1577754

WITHDRAWN

THE SHIP

THAT HELD UP

WALL STREET

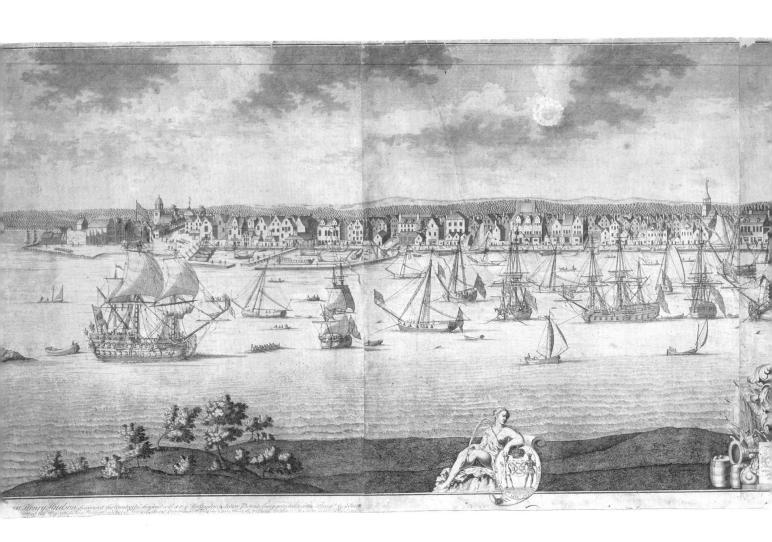

WARREN C. RIESS
WITH SHELI O. SMITH

The Ship
That Held Up
Wall Street

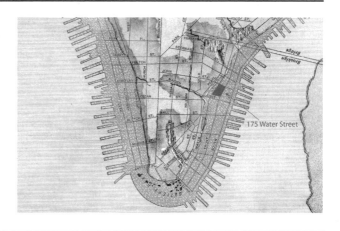

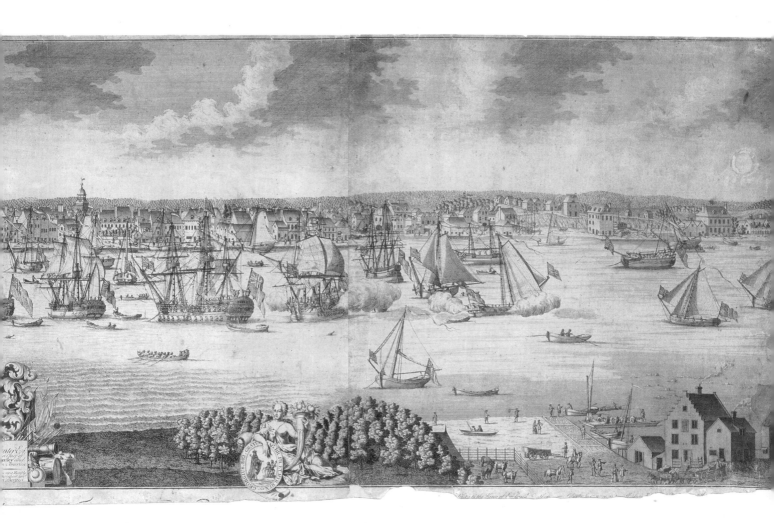

TEXAS A&M UNIVERSITY PRESS
College Station

Colorado College Library
Colorado Springs, Colorado

COPYRIGHT © 2015 BY WARREN C. RIESS
Manufactured in the United States of America
All rights reserved
First edition

This paper meets the requirements of ANSI/NISO z39.48-1992
(Permanence of Paper).
Binding materials have been chosen for durability.

Publication of this book was supported by a grant from
Furthermore: a program of the J. M. Kaplan fund.

DESIGNED BY TERESA W. WINGFIELD

LIBRARY OF CONGRESS CATALOGING-IN-PUBLICATION DATA

Riess, Warren, author.
 The Ship That Held Up Wall Street: / Warren C. Riess with
Sheli O. Smith. — First edition.
    pages cm — (Ed Rachal Foundation nautical
archaeology series)
  Includes bibliographical references and index.
  ISBN 978-1-62349-188-8 (hardback : alk. paper) —
  ISBN 978-1-62349-226-7 (ebook)
  1. Ronson Ship (Merchant ship: 18th century)
2. Excavations (Archaeology)—New York (State)—New
York. 3. Merchant ships—New York (State)—New York—
History—18th century. 4. Ships, Wooden—New York
(State)—New York—History—18th century. 5. Underwater
archaeology—New York (State)—New York. 6. Manhattan
(New York, N.Y.)—Antiquities. I. Smith, Sheli O.
II. Title. III. Title: Ship that Held Up Wall Street. IV. Series:
Ed Rachal Foundation nautical archaeology series.
  VM395.R66R55   2014
  910.9163'46   dc23
  2014012476

CONTENTS

PREFACE

On Tuesday evening, January 12, 1982, Sheli Smith and I received a call from New York that would change our lives. In the winter of 1981–82 we were two graduate students of maritime studies who had received our master's degrees in nautical archaeology from Texas A&M University. Sheli was applying to a PhD program at the University of Pennsylvania, while I was two years into studies for a PhD in history at the University of New Hampshire.

A land archaeology team had found a buried ship, there were then few people qualified to direct an archaeological ship investigation, and we were available. Before the month was over we were co-directing the excavation of an eighteenth-century merchant ship in Manhattan. For us the site was a major stroke of good fortune. Historians, archaeologists, and anthropologists had many questions about eighteenth-century ship design, construction, and uses. We were excited by the possibilities that the information from this site might offer.

A year later Sheli was focused on her graduate studies and a previous commitment to interpret key artifacts of the Revolutionary War privateer *Defence* site in Penobscot Bay, Maine. The investigation of the Manhattan ship site became the topic of my doctoral dissertation, and for the next twenty-eight years I intermittently continued the investigation—researching and analyzing the archaeological and historical data.

This is the story of the excavation and study of a colonial-era merchantman buried in Manhattan. With the help of Sheli and others I have aimed to present the story of this study as we lived it—uncovering data, avoiding or overcoming obstacles, and analyzing information from the site, laboratory, and archives. The archaeology, conservation, research, curation, and study of this ship took three decades and required the efforts of numerous people. I mention only a few in the text but have tried to thank all of them in acknowledgments.

In the first three chapters of this volume I explain how the ship was found, its possible significance to our understanding of the past, and how we obtained the archaeological data in a hurried winter excavation in Manhattan. Chapter 4 describes how we preserved the wood and other artifacts. In chapter 5 I offer a closer look at the physical remains of the ship, including a brief interpretation of its design and construction. Chapter 6 is a review of the methods and results of my attempt to identify the ship, and with that probable identification, in chapter 7 I present the history of the ship from its construction to its burial. In the last chapter I offer what we learned from the ship site about the methods and chronology of the development of Manhattan's 175 Water Street block.

Often in the text I use a plural personal pronoun because much of the site investigation was a team effort of two or more people. I conducted most of the historical research and much of the analysis, but for many of the tasks I was part of a larger team, so that the use of "we" and "our" is most appropriate. For this book, Sheli worked with me to write chapters 1 and 3, almost everything discussed in chapter 4 was under Betty Seifert's direction, and approximately half of chapter 8 is from the reports of Joan Geismar and other New York archaeologists. At the end of the volume is a glossary of technical terms cribbed mostly from that of J. Richard Steffy.

In this volume I have tried to use modern English,

except when it is best not to do so. For example, I use the modern name Charleston, South Carolina, rather than the original Charles Towne, and the English term flyboat, rather than the Dutch flute. As the book goes to press I am working on volume 2, which will be a close technical look at the ship's design and construction.

Readers familiar with publications about this site from the 1980s and 1990s will find some differences between them and my analyses and conclusions in the present work. The earlier conclusions were based on incomplete information and should be treated as preliminary.

ACKNOWLEDGMENTS

MANY PEOPLE have been part of this project since its inception. Howard Ronson and his associates, cognizant of the historic value of the site, supported the investigation well beyond any government or business requirements. The close cooperation of the people at HRO International, Fox and Fowle Architects, Soil Systems, George Fuller Construction Company, and the New York City Landmarks Preservation Commission supported the excavation, recording, analysis, and preliminary historical research for the ship and the recovery and conservation of the bow. The field crew, who accomplished the excavation under very harsh conditions, will always serve as an example of dedication overcoming adversity.

1982 Field Staff: Warren Riess and Sheli Smith, co-directors; Jay Cohen and Bertrand Herbert, crew chiefs; Robert Adams, Jay Allen, Thomas Amorosi, David Babsen, Kathy Biddick, Quentin Blaine, Debra Bodie, Eugene Boesch, Laurie Boros, Bobbi Lynn Brickman, Eric Clingen, Nicole Coolidge, Ellen Cosby, Ann Marie Cuskley, Valerie DeCarlo, Joseph Diamond, Anne Donadeo, Claire Falco, Andrea Foster, Elaine Friedman, Peggy Froeschauer, John Froeschauer, Edwina Gluck, Lisa Goldberg, Steven Gross, Laurel Harrison, Fred Harvey, Faith Hentshel, Peter Hentshel, Kerry Horn, Dana Howe, Abby Jaroslow, Sarah Keyishian, Marc Kodack, S. Ruby Lang, Jim Lally, Ann Marie Lunsford, Sam Margolin, Lee Margolis, Claudia Marshall, Barbara Mehrhof, H. James Merrick, William Moran, George Myers, Steven Nicklas, Philip Perazio, Valerie Perazio, Amy Pickell, Sissy Pipes, Jesse Ponz, Drew Pritsker, Keith Reiner, David Robinson, Julie Rosen, Jay Rosloff, Patricia Seabury, Richard Shallenberger, Scott Simpson, Annette Silver, Anne Somoroff, Ella Stewart, Barbara Stidworthy, Avery Stone, Richard Swete, and Debra Tiller.

Between May 1982 and May 1985 the constant attention of Heidi Miksch, Ken Morris, Betty Seifert, and Seifert's conservation staff guaranteed the preservation of the bow and many key artifacts. The gathering of remains, notes, photographs, and illustrations and the continued analysis and preservation of all the material has been made possible by the efforts of the board of directors, staff, and volunteers of the Mariners' Museum, especially by William Ackiss, Linda Brown, Kyle Conard, Gere Cobb, Al Foster, Anna Holloway, Ed Hoffman, Linda Kelsey, Richard Malley, George Matson, Lois Oglesby, Joe Powell, Virginia Powell, Linda Rogers, John Sands, Karen Shackelford, Paul Sullivan, William Wilkinson, and Jeanne Willoz-Egnor.

Helpful suggestions, encouragement, and guidance for the fieldwork, research, analysis and writing have come from many other people during the past thirty years, especially from George Bass, Robert Blanchette, Norman Brouwer, Charles Clark, Michael Cohen, Kevin Crisman, Christopher French, Amy Friedlander, David Hancock, Richard Jagels, David Lyon, David MacGregor, Charles Mazel, Elsie Morse, Kathleen Riess, Geoffrey Rossano, Darrett Rutman, MacClean Shakeshober, J. Richard Steffy, David Switzer, Patty Tennison, Peter Throckmorton, Ruth Turner, Walter Wales, Gordon Watts, David Wyman, and the editing staff of Texas A&M University Press.

My research was made possible with generous support from Betty Berry, the Mariners' Museum, the

National Maritime Historical Society, the Sydney Stern Foundation, and the University of Maine School of Marine Sciences. I am grateful for the very professional and friendly help I received from the library research staff members of the American Antiquarian Society, Archivo Nacional Torre do Tombo in Portugal, British National Archives, New-York Historical Society, South Carolina Historical Society, University of Virginia, and the Virginia Historical Society.

This book was only made possible by twenty-two years of encouragement, support, and editing from Kathleen.

THE SHIP
THAT HELD UP
WALL STREET

A Ship in Manhattan

LATE 1730S, MANHATTAN

On the east side of New York a small group of land-owners met, possibly looking out over the East River in front of their properties. The city had recently granted each of them the section of the East River across the street from their lot in order to create a new city block and allow ships and boats to approach a dry quay. If they accomplished the development within ten years they would each own a lot of new land, increasing their real estate. To save money and time they agreed to co-ordinate their efforts and bring in logs for cribbing and rocks, dirt, and trash-laden soil for fill to build the new land. As an outer wall for half of the block they decided to use a retired ship.

JANUARY 5, 1982, FINANCIAL DISTRICT
OF MANHATTAN

On Tuesday, as Fred Harvey slowly removed his backhoe's bucket from Deep Test No. 4, the eastern mud wall of the hole suddenly collapsed, revealing a large wooden structure. Archaeologists George Meyers and Bert Herbert took a close look, expecting to find more log cribbing similar to what they had seen else-where on the block. However, this wall was covered with horizontal planks, and the wall curved away from the hole as it descended into the earth. The three men exchanged looks: was this an old ship? If so, it was a wonderful discovery, but it came at a terrible time—the archaeologists were required to pack up and leave the block in just three weeks to make room for construc-tion crews.

Howard Ronson's HRO International, owner and developer of the block on which he intended to construct a thirty-story office building, had hired Soil Systems, Inc. (SSI) to conduct any research and tests that were required by the engineers, city, or state before construction. SSI in turn had hired Dr. Joan Geismar of New York City in 1981 to direct the re-quired archaeological investigation of the block. She began on October 30 with a crew of fifty-three people. Through November, December, and January Geismar's crew carefully excavated and recorded approximately one-sixth of the block, mostly former backyards located in the middle third of the block. For the rest of the block she chose four locations for "deep tests," wherein a backhoe operator excavated four-by-ten-foot trenches that were systematically sampled to recover artifacts and into which Bert Herbert descended to record the landfill levels and artifacts in each wall of the trench. That information would help Geismar understand how the rest of the block related to the one section she could study carefully. It was in the last planned trench, Deep Test No. 4, which she had chosen because it would contain the deepest landfill on the block, that they found the ship.

Within a week of the discovery Sheli Smith and I received a call from Jim Ahlberg, regional manager of SSI. "Can you come to Manhattan?" he asked, "We found an old ship." While both of us specialized in the nautical archaeology of colonial ships, I was the one available for a quick trip. Colonial merchant ships were my special interest, and less than a month earlier I had finished an in-depth study in graduate school of At-lantic ships and merchant shipping in the seventeenth and eighteenth centuries, so I felt well prepared.

I was only going to be in Manhattan for a day or two, so I packed a small bag with a notebook, camera,

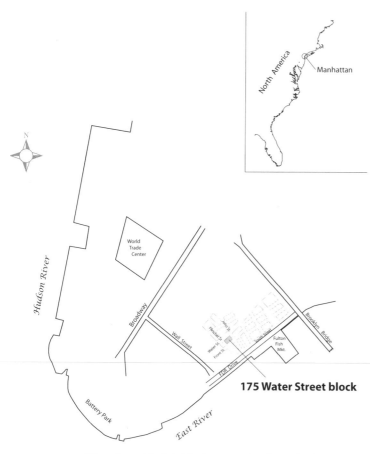

175 Water Street block in Manhattan, 1982. *Illustration by Warren Riess.*

while snowflakes would linger pleasantly on the fields and trees in Maine, I thought they would probably become a gray nuisance in one of the world's busiest cities. Two blocks inland from the East River in the Wall Street area the taxi stopped at a block surrounded by a twelve-foot-high plywood fence that was dwarfed by skyscrapers on three sides. I paid the cabbie and walked halfway around the block to find an insignificant door through the fence. Inside was a one-acre scene of many people industriously involved in archaeological tasks: digging, measuring, sketching, and photographing historic foundations and walls of logs. It reminded me of a Hollywood archaeology set, but this was not a sand-covered, sun-drenched Egyptian wasteland. The archaeologists here toiled in shin-deep mud, shadowed by office buildings, their clothing smudged with frozen mud.

Joan Geismar and Jim Ahlberg were there to meet me, but introductions had to be quick. Within five

one change of clothing, and rubber boots. The next morning I drove to the Portland Jetport before dawn and flew to JFK airport outside New York City. I was excited about the opportunity to see remains of the newly found colonial ship, if that was what had been found.

In San Francisco a few years earlier, construction excavators had unearthed a gold rush era ship. Because each day would cost the developer thousands of dollars for the construction crews and machinery to remain idle, archaeologists had been given less than a week to make a quick survey and save a section of the vessel before the rest was torn to pieces with construction machinery. I hoped to get a more detailed look at the New York ship but was prepared to make a quick survey if necessary.

From our phone conversation I was not sure where the site was in the city; I only had an address, which I gave to the cab driver at the airport while I regretted forgetting to bring a Manhattan street map. As I rode into the city, snow from a pending storm started to fall;

Bert Herbert offers the author an "elevator ride" into Deep Test No. 4 as a snowstorm begins. *Photo by Warren Riess, courtesy of the Mariners' Museum.*

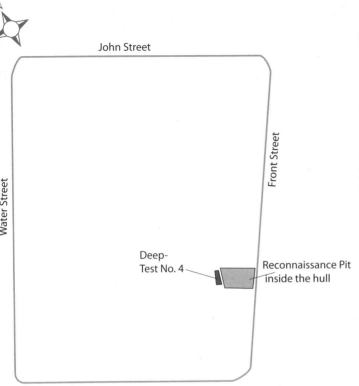

Site Map of 175 Water Street showing Deep Test No. 4 and the reconnaissance excavation within the hull. *Illustration by Warren Riess.*

minutes I stepped into a backhoe bucket that slowly lowered me into the Deep Test No. 4 hole. Heavy clouds and falling snow blocked the sun, making the interior of the wet trench quite dark. While my eyes adjusted, my face broadened into a smile as the outside of an old wooden ship's hull became apparent. From the type and size of the timbers, the position of a small gunport, and the fact that the planks were partially covered with animal hair, pitch, and wooden sheathing, I realized that this was a large eighteenth-century merchant ship. One of the first such ships to be found in the world, and possibly the best preserved, it appeared to be intact from a few feet above the lower deck down to the keel at the bottom of the ship.

Debbie Brodie, an archaeologist working on the site, joined me in the trench and we quickly measured and sketched what we could see of the vessel. Always conscious of being surrounded by ten feet of soft wet mud that could collapse at any moment, we worked rapidly. Debbie drew the overall structure, while I found and recorded details that were clues to the ship's identity and previous use. Among other things, I noticed that only a few boards of its thin outer sheathing remained,

suggesting to me that after its sailing days the ship had been laid up, possibly for years in the harbor, before being entombed.

My excitement grew as I contemplated the significance of the ship's remains. In December I had submitted a semester research paper in graduate school about the development of the British Empire in the first half of the eighteenth century. One of the key reasons for the empire's economic success was the halving of the expense of transatlantic shipping between 1713 and 1754. Several factors led to the lower cost, possibly including more economical ships; but until someone found and studied an early eighteenth-century British merchant ship, that remained only a hypothesis. Now, one month later, it appeared that I was looking at the outside of just such a ship. But what was it doing here?

Back at street level after two hours in the deep-test trench, I learned that Norman Brouwer, historian at the South Street Seaport Museum, had also identified the ship as a 1700s merchantman. This jogged my memory—Brouwer had written an article four years earlier about discovering that one of the museum's buildings was constructed directly on the remains of an old wooden ship. Unfortunately archaeologists were unable to investigate much of the ship without destabilizing the building's foundation. "Where is the museum from here?" I asked. It was only one block north of us. Joan, Jim, and I retreated to a warm, dry deli across the street to discuss the history of the site, the importance of the ship remains, and what should be done about this amazing find.

Over hot coffee and a pastry, Joan explained that the site had been a shallow portion of the East River that New Yorkers had filled in the mid-1700s. It became a commercial block supporting three-story buildings until the twentieth century, then served as a parking lot for a few years, and now HRO was sponsoring her archaeological investigation in preparation to construct a modern office building. She assumed the ship was part of the eighteenth-century filling process, but no one could be sure until someone took a more thorough look at it. Their contract with HRO, approved by the New York City Landmarks Preservation Commission, required all archaeology to cease on January 31. Since it would be necessary to construct the planned office building on hundreds of sixty-foot-long pilings, all archaeological remains, including the ship, would be quickly destroyed, removed, and trucked away. Joan and Jim asked me how important I thought the ship's remains might be.

IN AMERICA'S COLONIAL PERIOD numerous merchant ships were plying the oceans as the foremost means of communications among the peoples of the world. From the beginning of civilization to the mid-twentieth century, merchant ships were the carriers of people, culture, raw materials, manufactured goods, food, news, and disease between communities separated by large bodies of water. Even for communities connected by land, travel and communication by ships and coastal boats was often faster, safer, and less expensive than by land.

To a developing colonial empire, merchant ships were the equivalent of red blood cells in an adolescent human. Red blood cells move to all living cells of a body to provide nutrients and oxygen in exchange for waste or surplus material. Efficient red blood cells help a young body stay healthy and grow. In the eighteenth century, the more efficiently merchant ships could transport necessary cargo to various parts of an empire, the healthier would be the empire and the faster it could expand.

A better understanding of the transatlantic vessels' designs and an evaluation of their efficiency would provide important insight into the colonial period, for overseas trade helped shape the economic history of the British Empire, including its American colonies. Unfortunately however, merchant ships lacked the glamor to capture the imagination of either eighteenth-century or modern readers and writers. As a result we knew little about them.

Historians have rarely considered colonial era merchant ships as anything other than wooden containers that ferried people and cargo to and from various places. This superficial treatment comes more from a lack of surviving records than from a lack of professional interest. The paucity of surviving documents is probably due to the low priority eighteenth-century clerks gave to creating and preserving records on such a mundane subject. Even with today's interest in the preservation of records, only a few repositories preserve information concerning modern merchantmen.

Archival information on early eighteenth-century transatlantic ships was limited to registration records of port officials, a few visual representations that show the upper works and hulls of various ships, and few written descriptions. The only known detailed illustrations of eighteenth-century merchantmen were published in Sweden by Fredrik Chapman in 1768.[1]

Archaeological evidence in 1982 also was meager. Due to a lack of protective legislation, would-be treasure salvors were destroying many colonial ship sites underwater and previous construction had destroyed a few in harbors. Nautical archaeologists, by chance and preference, had investigated only a few colonial era merchant vessels worldwide, mostly underwater with a few buried in ports, and none were the common British transatlantic cargo carriers of the early eighteenth century.

The ship that lay buried at 175 Water Street was a possible source of heretofore unknown information about eighteenth-century commercial vessels and the people who designed, built, owned, sailed, and used them. I felt certain that we could extricate information from the site that would help us understand the design, construction, and utility of merchant ships; we might also gain insight into the colonial merchant trade in general. Were we to determine this ship's identity, we could learn more precisely the role it played in America's early trade and the British Empire's expansion.

I replied to Joan and Jim, "Very important." They listened to my reasoning, discussed my comments for a short time, and then agreed. Given that at this point no one knew how much remained of the ship or possible cargo within it, they requested, and quickly received HRO's and the New York City Landmarks Preservation Commission's permission to carefully conduct a ten-by-ten-foot reconnaissance excavation within the hull of the ship during the remaining two weeks of January, before construction crews were due on the site. Our hope was that we could learn enough to determine properly whether a more thorough investigation of the ship would be worth the necessary resources. I called home for Sheli to join us as soon as possible, repeating, "It's the whole side of the ship!" Then I checked in at the Vista Hotel at the World Trade Center.

That night I had dinner with Jim and afterward, in the midst of the snow storm, we enjoyed ourselves taking in the sights and having a couple of drinks along Manhattan's then notorious 42nd Street. To relieve daytime tension, businessmen like to keep "off the clock" conversations to anything but business, which is what we did too. But it was not easy, for as our daughter would say, archaeologists are both blessed and cursed with a passion. We have no off hours. We want to talk about interesting finds, research, and analyses

The reconnaissance excavation inside ship's hull, just before finding the ship's lower deck. *Photo by Warren Riess, courtesy of the Mariners' Museum.*

all the time. A buried ship was taunting me with a probable treasure trove of significant information, and I was eager to make the site the topic of conversation. I had to bite my tongue through the entire evening.

Snow blanketed Manhattan the next morning, yet everything in the city seemed to be running on schedule. Not much could slow the industrious New Yorkers. I arrived at the site to begin excavating inside the ship's hull. Eight feet of twentieth- and nineteenth-century rubble covered the ship's remains, and we needed to remove it quickly to study the ship. Joan told me she would have Fred Harvey, one of the heavy equipment operators at the site, do so with his backhoe. Having only experienced backhoes being used to dig crude irrigation holes and trenches quickly, I shook my head and told her no backhoe should get within four feet of the ship's fragile timbers. Without saying another word to me, she asked Fred to use his backhoe to pick up a particular ceramic shard off a foundation wall twenty feet away and put it in my hand. With consummate delicacy he picked it up with one of the bucket's teeth, swung his machine's arm in a graceful arc, and gently placed it in my open palm.

An hour later Fred had cleared away the surface layer of pavement and the underlying eight feet of rubble with his backhoe, just to the east of Deep Test No. 4, where I thought we would be within the ship's hull. Bert Herbert, George Myers, and I initiated our excavation with shovels and trowels using standard archaeological methods. We quickly found four large oak deck beams and a supporting oak hanging knee (see glossary). Below them was a layer of white coral sand and below that was a layer of granite cobblestones. It looked as if we were indeed within the hull, which had possibly been filled with excess ballast from other ships. Just a few small eighteenth-century ceramic shards were mixed in the sand and cobble layers.

During the second day of excavating the reconnaissance pit, just as Sheli arrived from Maine, we uncovered a deck within the ship, twelve feet below the present street level. We were elated. The deck was made of hard pine planks, eight to ten inches wide. It appeared to be the lower of two decks on the ship, for it was approximately four feet below the deck beam and knee found on the first day. We estimated that this vessel was probably intact from five feet above the waterline to the keel.

Within the first week of excavation the square pit

A Ship in Manhattan 5

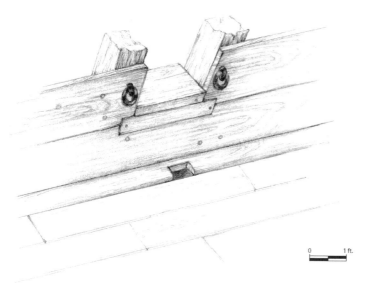

Illustration of the gunport, as it probably was when in use. The wrought iron rings, used to secure the ends of a recoil rope, were attached to the hull with large wrought iron staples. *Illustration by Kathleen Galligan.*

revealed much more of the hull. A small gunport, designed to allow a cannon to fire through the hull, was on the western side. An iron ring was fastened to either side of the gunport with a large wrought iron staple. Sailors used these rings to anchor the retaining lines and tackle for the cannon. On the east side of the pit was a stanchion protruding from a large cargo hatch in the deck. This stanchion, sometimes called a monkey pole, was used both to support a deck beam at the hatch and to provide a climbing pole for the crew. It was notched approximately every fifteen inches for steps. Also on the deck was a smaller hatch that had been planked-over some time before the ship had been buried.

By measuring from the notched stanchion, assumed to be in the center of the ship, to the outside of the hull, we calculated that the ship had a beam (maximum width) of approximately 25 feet. Since most eighteenth-century ships had a length-to-breadth ratio of between 3 and 4 to 1, the vessel probably had a length of 75 to 100 feet. We thought the ship was probably distorted from many years under many feet of fill and three-story buildings, but it was remarkably intact compared to the ship remains we normally encountered in underwater archaeology sites. The hull's orientation indicated that it lay on an approximate north-south axis, with its western side in the 175 Water Street block and its eastern side, and most of its southern end, under Front Street. At that time, and for several

more days, we found no clues to indicate whether its bow was at the north or south end.

As we talked with other archaeologists and members of the construction crew they told us of other old ships found a few years earlier on a construction site three blocks from us. Heavy equipment operators who were clearing the block for a new building there found the remains of four wooden ships that seemed to have been brought in as fill for that block. New York preservation laws and attitudes had been different then. Though the crew stopped to take a quick look, they were under a tight schedule. Within hours they had reduced the ships to broken timbers, to be hauled away and used as fill elsewhere.

We realized that the vessel at 175 Water Street, entombed for more than two hundred years, was the first major discovery of a colonial merchant ship that had a chance to be thoroughly studied, and we were thrilled by the rare extent of its preservation. Not only was there a great quantity of the ship left, but what remained had been well protected from deterioration by a dense mud. The wood was in relatively good shape; even tool marks left by the shipwrights' hand tools could be seen on sections of the wood's surface. However, only one week remained before the archaeological deadline when the ship would be destroyed. We knew there was no chance of gathering enough information to determine the ship's design, construction, or identity in only one week. Sheli and I determined to ask for more time.

Aware that any delays would cost HRO thousands of dollars a day in February, and that on March 1 the developer's costs would increase by a factor of five, we needed a plan that would be thorough and quick. Over meals and in the evenings Sheli and I began to calculate how to excavate and record the ship during the twenty-eight days of February. Neither of us had rushed an excavation before; usually archaeologists had months if not years for site investigations.

While archaeology is often the only way to discover certain information about our past, it is sometimes a difficult science. The ethics of archaeology differ from and demand more than those in most scientific endeavors. In most sciences, other people can replicate an experiment or obtain a new sample to test someone's conclusions. Unfortunately, archaeologists need to destroy each layer of a site or excavation pit before they can excavate the next layer. Consequently, no one else ever will be able to look at or study the destroyed layer. Eventually we destroy the entire site. It is therefore imperative that before we start to excavate a site we not only develop a plan to extract and record the most information possible but also that we plan a full site investigation.

A site investigation includes every stage from its discovery through a final publication. Archaeologists therefore need to commit themselves conscientiously to complete a site's analysis, interpretation, and publication. As professional as our records might be, no one else will be able to study any details and relationships that do not get recorded, yet are important in the final analysis of a site. The average time from the start of excavation to the finished site publication is fifteen years. If all went well, Sheli and I were going to be entrusted with the investigation of an extremely important colonial site. Our first challenge was to develop quickly a research design that would satisfy our ethics and the needs of the developer.

Nature, people, and simple mistakes often hamper excavation and recording operations. These are typical for any archaeological investigation, but a rapid, quickly planned excavation in New York City in February would be a magnet for problems that would have to be overcome. Flexible was the key word in all our initial and subsequent planning. Sheli and I decided to split the directorship so that I would concentrate on the excavation and general interactions with Soil Systems and the construction company, while she concentrated on the many aspects of recording the site and preserving the artifacts as well as some ship timbers. At least one of us would be on the site at all times so that field operations could continue should the other be supervising laboratory work, attending a meeting, or dealing with unforeseen necessities.

Our field plan called for a large crew to be split into four groups: an excavation team of thirty-five people; a wood recording team of four, who measured, sketched, and photographed each timber or plank as it was removed from the site; a hull recording team of four; and a support staff of three. We planned for a six-day workweek through February to excavate and record the ship. Since the site was almost entirely below the water table, we would ask for three portable water and mud pumps to keep the site drained. Besides normal archaeological equipment, we needed two backhoes with the best professional operators to clear the overlying frozen pavement and rubble and after that to perform as portable cranes on the site to lift and relocate heavy timbers and large buckets of hand-excavated fill.

Since the rest of the archaeological excavation in the block was coming to an end, we assumed we could hire most of our crew from those highly experienced people who were mostly professional archaeologists and historians. In addition, we would need a few people who, like us, specialized in nautical archaeology. They would be coming in fresh to a harsh environment, but underwater archaeologists are accustomed to working accurately and deftly in difficult environments. February in Manhattan would not present ideal excavation and recording conditions, but we naively thought it would be much easier than our usual underwater archaeology sites along the coast of Maine, where we often worked in zero-visibility, frigid water.

As the day approached for the critical meeting that would decide the fate of the ship, we made contingency plans just in case we were not granted the one month and funds we thought a minimum to complete a rapid excavation. If we were granted only the few days left until the end of January, we would continue to excavate the section we had started, try to locate the north end, and do our best to record what we could of it. If we were granted the time and funds for two weeks of February, we would use what crew we could afford to complete our first section and study both ends of the ship.

Apprehension filled our minds as I presented our plan to representatives of Soil Systems, HRO, and the Landmarks Commission at an afternoon meeting on January 28. These were friendly and intelligent but quite powerful people. Would they entrust this important site investigation to two graduate students? After I finished, there were only a few minutes of questions and deliberation, in which I realized why these people had risen in ranks to be at the conference table. While each needed to ensure that a particular corporation's or institution's interests were covered, they focused their attention and ingenuity to reach a consensus about how to proceed. Fairly quickly they all agreed to grant us the permission, the month of February, and the resources necessary to excavate and record that part of the ship not directly under Front Street and its sidewalk.

The rest of the meeting was more than positive. Bob Fox, HRO's representative and architect for the new building, made it clear to Sheli and me that Howard Ronson wanted the excavation and subsequent analysis and interpretation to be conducted at the highest level of professional standards, not minimal acceptable standards. Fox stressed the importance of finishing on time, and since HRO was footing the bill, we took his advice to hire more archaeologists than we thought we needed, rent extra pumps, hire a dedicated pump operator, and take other backup precautions to keep the operation flowing even when the inevitable problems arose.

Joan Geismar, as archaeological director of the entire 175 Water Street project, agreed we could work independently on the ship remains while she continued to direct the block's massive terrestrial site investigation. Soil Systems committed to streamline the administration by having Pat Garrow, their chief archaeologist, stay in New York as site manager to interface with HRO, the Landmarks Commission, and the press and to expedite financial necessities. In addition, Dr. Sherene Baugher Perlman, archaeologist at the Landmarks Commission, cleared her calendar for the next month to help make the excavation successful.

Our proposal had come to life; Sheli and I were to co-direct the archaeological fieldwork and I would take the lead in later tasks of the investigation as she was already committed to another important project. I had also asked if I could conduct the associated historical research and publication for my Ph.D. dissertation in history at the University of New Hampshire. That decision was left to Dr. Amy Friedlander, senior historian with Soil Systems. When she found that my Ph.D.

committee chair was Darrett Rutman, whom she considered an excellent historian and a highly critical and demanding professor, she gave her blessing.

Sheli and I had been given a rare gift—an important site to co-direct, with the time and funding we had requested. We also had the ethical and contractual responsibility to do the best possible job. Both of us were happy, yet knowing there were many challenges ahead, we were also focused and determined.

The next day our two highly skilled backhoe operators began to clear six to eight feet of frozen asphalt, concrete, and nineteenth-century building rubble that lay over the ship. Jay Cohn and Bert Herbert, chosen to be our two new crew chiefs, started recruiting New York area archaeologists for the team—mostly people who were about to finish Joan Geismar's terrestrial archaeology excavation. I began calling nautical archaeologists to fill some ship-specific positions. We needed a name for the ship site but did not know the vessel's eighteenth-century name. Therefore, following one archaeological tradition, Sheli and I named the site after the current landowner: it became the Ronson ship site.

In three days we would start the full-scale operation to learn as much as possible about this ship that New Yorkers had buried so many years before. We had many details to plan and arrange.

Atlantic and Manhattan History

Aꜱʏɴᴛʜᴇᴛɪᴄ ᴡᴏʀʟᴅ completely surrounds one in Manhattan. When I visited New York City before 1982, walking along its sidewalks I found it easy to shift from feeling relatively normal in my horizontal plane at street level to feeling slightly claustrophobic and rather small among the immense buildings towering above, occupied by thousands of people. Occasionally I contemplated the obscured network of the industrious world below my feet. Under the sidewalks, streets, and buildings, layers of tunnels for subways and storm drainage intertwined with pipes for natural gas, water, and sewage; cables for electric power and communications; and spaces for basements, vaults, and transit terminals. Never had I considered the natural world of Manhattan as it existed before humans arrived. Not once had it occurred to me there could exist remains of nature and early humans buried below modern New York. Hadn't all of that been scraped away, down to bedrock, to make way for this massive city?

The bedrock of Manhattan is a hilly granite outcrop left in place by a series of glaciers that scoured and eroded the softer rock around the granite, to form the Hudson River, the East River, and New York Harbor. Approximately ten miles long and one mile wide, the island forms the east bank of the mouth of the Hudson River, the west bank of the East River (actually an estuary), and the south bank of the Harlem River, a branch of the Hudson. During the approximately eleven thousand years after the last glacier receded, tundra, then forests and open grass areas developed, slowly creating and improving the island's topsoil.

Manhattan is surrounded by water, which before the nineteenth century was teaming with finfish and shellfish. Its position at the intersection of the sizeable Hudson River, many estuaries and marshes, and the ocean is a perfect place for fish to breed, mature, and feed. The prevailing winds are westerlies, blowing surface water east across the Atlantic. Water from the deep Atlantic replaces that surface water by sweeping across the bottom of the continental shelf, carrying many important nutrients into the estuaries and marshes surrounding the island. Plankton, the foodstuff of most small sea life, use the nutrients to proliferate, creating a food cornucopia for small sea life in the estuaries, including oysters, clams, and mussels. For millennia these mollusks, and the large finfish that ate the small fish and mollusks, filled the nearby waters in numbers that are almost inconceivable today. They could and did feed human populations there for thousands of years.

Archaeologists have found evidence of people living on Manhattan soon after the last glacier had left the island. These first settlers found an island almost surrounded by intertidal mud flats and shallow water that one would have to traverse to gain access to the deeper river channels. Thousands of years later, the last tribal people to live on Manhattan were the Munsee, part of the Lenape people. Anthropologists are not sure if the Munsee were the original humans to migrate into the area or if they replaced an earlier group. Evidence indicates that those living on Manhattan and the land around it lived in small villages, with many intersecting paths that allowed easy foot transportation. These people supplemented a diet of fish and animals with garden-grown and gathered vegetation. With a plethora of seafood, the Munsee and their possible predecessors had no need for the more work-intensive maize-based diet of the inland agricultural people.[1]

Wherever they were able, be it on lake, river, or ocean, Native Americans used canoes for transportation that involved long distances or heavy cargo. In Manhattan pre-contact sites archaeologists have found evidence of trade along the coast and inland—tools and weapons made of material not natural to the region.[2] From the east came European explorers, traders, and settlers. With their dependence on fishing, use of water transportation, and familiarity with trade, the indigenous people of Manhattan had some commonalities with the Europeans who established a settlement on the island in the early seventeenth century. Complex forces in Europe would bring many of the new settlers into the Munsees' world.

Throughout the sixteenth century most of the world was in turmoil. While China seemed stable from afar, internal and external forces constantly challenged the empire's solidity. India, historically Hindu, had been invaded by Mongols in the north and was split into many rival principalities, their people divided into thousands of social castes. Africa was thinly populated, and being probed by European traders seeking profitable trade. Concurrently, at times due to their failures and successes abroad, Europeans frequently warred, coerced, and plotted against one another. Rulers knew they had to thrive to survive. Once strong they could gain strength by conquering and absorbing weaker rivals. Portugal and then Spain developed ways to create and enlarge overseas empires to increase their economies and thus allow them to afford expanded armies and navies.

The American continents and islands had been populated by people of many cultures, whose means of survival, relationships to one another, and religions varied widely. Into this world sailed Spanish adventurers, who conquered and settled the larger Caribbean islands, Middle America, and important regions of South America. In the sixteenth century only the Spanish developed permanent colonies in the Americas, though other Europeans occasionally tried unsuccessfully to do so. A number of Europeans were exploring the North American continent, searching for a navigable northern passage to Asia to establish direct trade with the East.

By the beginning of the seventeenth century European attitudes toward North America underwent a significant shift in perception. No longer considered an obstacle to direct Asian trade, the continent offered instead the possibility of a fertile region on which to establish trading and fishing settlements. Some

Europeans also were more than a little interested in establishing settlements to extract timber and other "naval stores" from North America's vast forests. Such resources were especially important to the English, whose national welfare and defense depended on their merchant and naval ships, while their own forests were becoming depleted. In addition, the English had a growing overpopulation problem. For these reasons northern Europeans began to reacquaint themselves with earlier explorers' charts and notes and launched exploratory expeditions to find the best spots for trading, fishing, timber production, and farming settlements.

In North America, Manhattan Island sat just north of the fortieth parallel, at about the same latitude as Madrid in Spain, and Naples in Italy. While the island was cooler than those locations, its proximity to the Atlantic Ocean provided comfortable weather throughout most of the year. The growing season was approximately five months, plenty of time to grow one planting of most American and European crops in the fertile soil. Winters were mild compared to New England, offering ice-free conditions in the deep harbor through most, but not all, winters.

To seventeenth-century Europeans, Manhattan's geography suggested a promising natural bastion from which one could control water transportation in the region. Its fertile, hilly terrain offered reasonable farming and good residential property to support a large trading settlement. The land was surrounded by water, which offered fish for food and which hindered infantry attacks, yet it was protected by Long Island and Staten Island from the direct assault of ocean waves and surprise water-borne attacks. Manhattan's ten-mile western shoreline, which formed the southernmost east bank of the Hudson River, allowed almost complete control of water access to the vast hinterland served by the river. Small vessels could move cargo from the upper regions of the river system to Manhattan, or shippers might transfer their cargo at Albany to ocean-sailing ships. In either case, whoever held Manhattan controlled the trade of the interior. In addition, as the European colonies developed, New York was geographically central to the North American colonies. Coastal trade between the middle colonies could be protected or harassed by government or private warships operating out of the harbor.

On Manhattan, water transportation routes to the ocean were through one of two natural channels. The

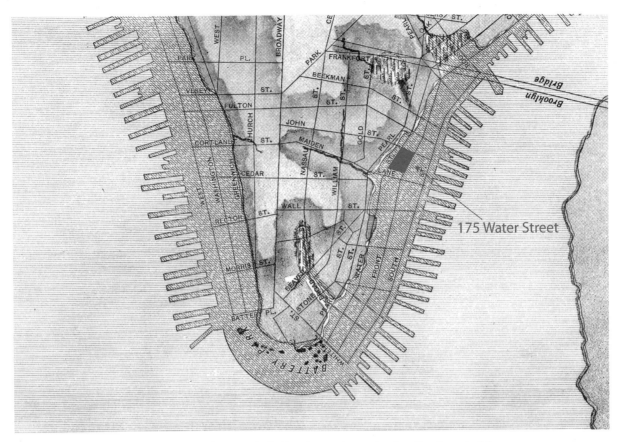

175 Water Street

Aerial view of Lower Manhattan, showing the natural island and extensions to its shoreline through 1867.
Townsend MacCoun, 1909.

safer passage was south between Staten Island and Long Island, then close to Sandy Point, New Jersey, and out into the Atlantic Ocean. The other passage ran up the East River, through the narrows and Hell Gate between Long Island and the mainland, into Long Island Sound, and eventually out into the Atlantic around the eastern end of Long Island or nearby Fishers Island or Block Island.

Its unique combination of weather, soil, position, and surrounding waterways made Manhattan one of the most promising locations for the development of a European trade settlement in the seventeenth century. Only the island's surrounding mud flats, which held large ships approximately two hundred yards off the shore, prevented it from being a perfect natural trading port for transatlantic ships.

Although Verrazano had explored the region in 1524, the first significant European contact with the island was the entrance into the lower bay of Henry Hudson's *Half Moon* on September 12, 1609. Hudson was searching for the elusive Northwest Passage for

the Dutch East India Company. He reported the local resources and possibility of fur trading with the local natives. However, the Dutch East India Company was intently focused on the Asian trade, so they did not pursue his suggestion. Instead, smaller entrepreneurs began trading expeditions to the Hudson River until the newly incorporated Dutch West India Company provided the necessary collective funds to establish a trading settlement along the Hudson River. It was necessary to advance at a pace as the English settlements were spreading north from Virginia and south from Massachusetts. In 1624 the Dutch West India Company established Orange (modern Albany), farther up the river. Two years later the company established the settlement of New Amsterdam on the southern tip of Manhattan.

The Dutch West India Company's main interest in colonizing North America was trade with the native population. They needed a deep water port for gathering and distributing, importing and exporting goods—an entrepôt. To this end their choice of Manhattan was

A view of Manhattan in the Dutch period, c. 1679–1680. Note the log cribbing at the high tide line. Detail from *The Labadist General View of New York* (Jasper Danckaerts, 1679–80). *Collection of the New York Public Library, image 53907.*

excellent. The large island was at the mouth of a long, navigable river that provided both native and Dutch transportation into an extensive hinterland abundant with furs. Transatlantic Dutch vessels could enter and sail from the entrepôt without much difficulty. All these factors allowed for the relatively inexpensive transportation of furs and later agricultural products from the Hudson River to the company's warehouses in Europe.[3]

During the first half century, the Dutch spent much of their collective effort on municipal construction endeavors. They paved only one street, aptly named Stone Street, yet built a fort, converted a creek into a canal, and made substantial improvements to the harbor facilities. Most of their projects were not technically innovative, as the Dutch used standard engineering practices for port cities throughout the developed world. However, their industries demonstrated a desire to develop New Amsterdam into a permanent entrepôt for the New World. The Dutch built piers, constructed retaining walls at the high water mark to inhibit erosion around the town, and filled behind the walls to establish a low quay that almost surrounded the southern end of the island. Evidence from several New York archaeology sites indicates that the Dutch generally used a crib of horizontal logs secured by vertical piles at the quay.[4]

Cargoes were moved from and to ships by scows (flat-bottomed boats) or directly from small vessels that could beach close to the quays at high tide or navigate the canal at what is now Broad Street. In 1658 the Dutch constructed a large basin called *the stone dock* along the southeastern shoreline, to accommodate medium to large ships. It was a body of water that they almost enclosed with stone-filled log cribbing, allowing ships and storage hulks to float in a protected area.[5]

Throughout the seventeenth century England and the Netherlands vacillated between being allies and enemies. At times they fought alongside each other against their common enemy, Spain. However, the English and Dutch, as economic rivals, fought each other in several wars as they developed overseas trade and empires. In the 1660s they were in the midst of one of the wars that would determine control of trade in various parts of the world. In North America the Dutch intention for New Amsterdam was different from that of the English, who were establishing farming settlements to the north and south of the Dutch. While English settlements quickly grew into heavily populated colonies, Manhattan remained a poorly fortified but successful trading settlement throughout much of the 1600s. The Dutch settlement in America was a rival and danger to the English settlements, and yet it had the potential to be an important trading and shipping center in England's expanding North American holdings.

On September 8, 1664, the Dutch surrendered New Amsterdam without a fight to a small but powerful English squadron. From that day forward, with the exception of Dutch control regained for just shy of a year in 1673–74, the city, renamed New York, remained English until the American Revolution. Under the rule of English governor Edmund Andros, the New Yorkers, a mixture of Dutch, English, and other nationalities, expanded the city's trade and port facilities. Among the improvements was a new basin that was completed in 1675. Manhattan's commercial role continued to be as the trading station for New York's interior with Europe and the West Indies. As immigrants moved into the New York interior and cleared the region for agriculture, the colony's exports slowly shifted from furs to flour, other agricultural goods, and timber products. By 1720 the colony of New York's farming communities had expanded enough to produce significant amounts of export goods. Eventually, new milling and bolting (flour sifting) laws added quality control to the flour export trade, enhancing it substantially, while the fur trade gradually played a smaller but still vibrant role.[6]

Shipping activities grew markedly in the eighteenth century, and the people of Manhattan continued the expansion of their land into the shallow water around them. The city's commercial and shipping activities were mainly along the shore of the East River. In 1716 a visitor recorded that "a fine quay . . . reigns all around the town, built with stone and piers of wood outside. There are small docks [berths] for cleaning and building small ships. At high water, the vessels come up to the quay to lade and unlade."[7]

As the port expanded, merchants employed larger, more economical commercial ships in the transatlantic trade. Colonial New York port records show that prior to 1720 few merchant ships entering the port were registered at more than 100 tons. But in the next few years the larger ships became more common.[8] Since New York possessed a good harbor centrally located in the thirteen colonies, it also was used by the British (Great Britain was created from England, Scotland, and Wales in 1703) as an important military terminal.[9] A 1717 view of New York from the Brooklyn Heights depicts many merchantmen and warships anchored in the East River.[10]

With new settlers immigrating into and being born in the colony, the colonists were converting what had been a small trading settlement into a significant commercial city in the New World, with a population of approximately seven thousand people by 1720. This small number of people accomplished much to enhance their physical and commercial environment.

As the city expanded north of Wall Street in the mid-1700s, the merchants there filled in the mud flats and shallow waters of the East River's shore and constructed commercial buildings on the new land. A series of maps of New York indicates that developers filled outward from the original shoreline to what became Water Street, then filled in the 175 Water Street block between 1745 and 1755.[11] The block supported new commercial buildings on its west side, while its east side served as a road and the new quay for the East River. Between 1773 and 1810 construction crews filled the shallow water of the river outward another block, leaving the 175 Water Street block approximately 250 feet from the new waterfront.

Eventually, small buildings occupied the entire block. They were generally commercial and residential in nature, having shops on the ground level and residential units in the upper floors. For more than a century the block remained part of the waterfront commercial area, with a mixture of fish markets, chandleries, wholesalers, retailers, and related services. From the late 1800s to the 1950s the block was occupied by light industry and warehouse businesses. Between 1956 and 1960 the owners razed the buildings and

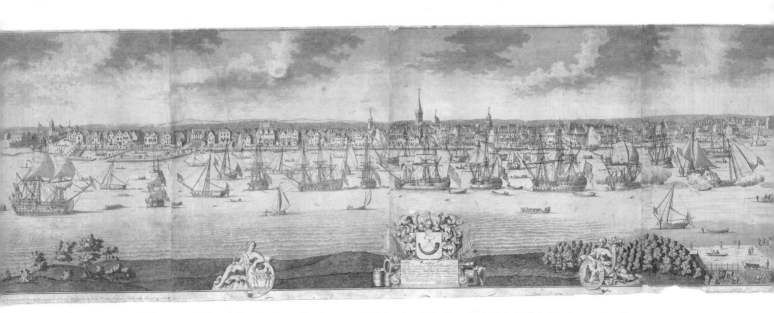

A view of New York from Brooklyn Heights (William Burgis, c. 1717). *Collection of the New-York Historical Society, image 32098.*

paved the block to create a parking lot for the Financial District.

It was in 1981 that Howard Ronson's HRO International, a British development firm, purchased the parking lot to construct a thirty-story office building. Since the lot is in a historic district, the New York City Landmarks Preservation Commission required HRO to conduct a historical and archaeological study of the block. Because of time constraints and the high costs involved, the approved research design called for Soil Systems to conduct a careful archaeological investigation of approximately one-sixth of the block and four deep test trenches in the remaining area to compare the stratigraphy found throughout the site.

The archaeological clause of the permit contract stated: "An archaeological survey will be undertaken at the sole expense of the Applicant and/or his successors in interest to evaluate the historical significance of the construction site. The survey will encompass the following elements . . . Field Research through testing to determine if any artifacts or other items of significance, such as house foundations, wells, privies or even sunken ships, are contained within the selected areas."

February, Major Excavation Operations

On a brisk Monday, February 1, our crew of forty-six people assembled at the site to begin the month-long task of excavating and recording the ship. They were a mixed group of bright young men and women—mostly New York area archaeologists and historians with at least a bachelor's degree and experience in archaeological investigations. They were enthusiastic about the opportunity to assist in studying this unique find, though few of them had prior experience on a ship site. Most of the crew had just labored through the weekend to finish the excavation of the rest of the 175 Water Street block. They were tired after six months of hard, precise work, efficiently excavating and recording the wet, muddy sites at 155 John Street with Diana Wall and then 175 Water Street with Joan Geismar.

In addition to local archaeologists we recruited six nautical archaeologists. Five were students and graduates of our alma mater, the Nautical Archaeology program at Texas A&M University: Jay Rosloff and Ruby Lang led the wood recording team, Bob Adams recorded the ship photographically, while Sam Margolin and Dick Swete helped with excavation and recording the ship's lines. Quentin Blaine joined us from the University of New Hampshire to be the occasional carpenter, purchaser, and social conscience in crew matters.

With the excavation crew divided into five teams, Bert Herbert supervised three teams and Jay Cohen supervised two, providing direction and standardization throughout the site. While we supervised, the true expediters of the site were the thirty-six individual archaeologists excavating and recording under adverse weather conditions in the ship's deep hull. As almost everyone on the team was either a professional or graduate student in archaeology, their innovative ideas often solved small problems before they grew large.

Most of the excavation crew in early February. The entire crew is listed in the acknowledgments. Sheli Smith is front row, second from the right; Joan Geismar is second row, first on the right; Warren Riess is last row, first on the right. *Photo by Drew Pritzker, courtesy of the Mariners' Museum.*

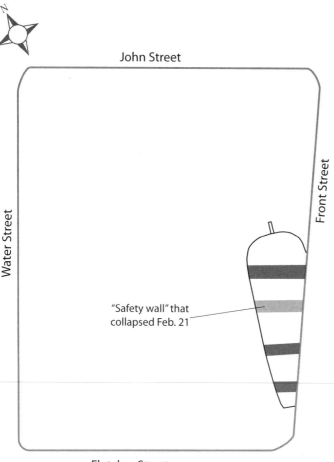

John Street

Water Street

Front Street

"Safety wall" that
collapsed Feb. 21

Fletcher Street

175 Water Street block with an outline of the ship and the lot walls we were required to leave in place "to support the ship's hull." *Illustration by Warren Riess.*

Overseeing all the archaeology at 175 Water Street was Pat Garrow, the site project manager for Soil Systems. Besides conferring with us at least daily, he provided an "umbrella" to protect us from outside problems, dealing with SSI headquarters, HRO, George Fuller Construction, local authorities, and the press. When we needed something outside the norm, he provided the means to obtain it. He worked tirelessly on and off the site to offer suggestions, facilitate the project, and allow us to concentrate on our job of uncovering and recording the ship.

Certain diversions from normal archaeology procedures were necessary because of the winter weather and limited time frame we had to complete the fieldwork. To protect the crew from freezing rain and snow, Fuller Construction erected a large awning that could be collapsed when necessary. HRO paid for hard hats, ear plugs, and foul weather outerwear for each crew member. Two backhoes with cables and hooks would act as small mobile cranes. We purchased a gross (144) of five-gallon pickle buckets to facilitate fill removal, a dozen rolls of duct tape, every garden hose Quentin could find in Manhattan, and a chainsaw with five extra chains. A large truckload of salt marsh hay from Long Island helped insulate exposed timber from freezing air at night. Foresight and many such small innovations kept the project humming.

As we began to dig by hand within the ship, we realized that although the nineteenth-century buildings had been razed in the 1950s and 1960s, their foundations still lay over the ship, their walls running across the hull, athwartships. The nineteenth-century builders of these structures placed the foundation footers atop the remaining deck beams of this ship. Concerned that the footers were the only things keeping the ship from collapsing, SSI's safety engineers felt that we should leave the walls in place to help prevent the sides of the ship from falling in on us while we excavated. Physically restrained from inspecting the whole ship, we excavated between the old foundations, adopting the street numbers of the former buildings to designate the excavation units on the vessel. The bow was to the north, in Lot 31, and the stern to the south, in Lot 35.

The ship was oblique to Front Street, with the starboard side, from twenty feet aft of the bow, beneath the sidewalk and street. To excavate the starboard side would have cost a fortune in time and would have forced the closing of businesses along Front Street. It might also have been a futile endeavor since earlier construction of water, sewer, and power lines under the street might already have destroyed any remains of that portion of the ship. Ships are generally symmetrical, and we were planning to examine the entire port side and bow of the vessel. Under the circumstances, missing the starboard side seemed to be a reasonable loss.

Into the persistently grueling winter weather the excavation crew systematically shoveled, troweled, and recorded down through the fill in the ship. After a week, on February 5 we could see the tops of the ship's oak frames, defining the approximately ninety-foot long outline of all of the ship that remained in the block. Instead of being sharp, as in a modern ship, the bow was very full, almost square in appearance at the top. Protruding in front of it was a beak or knee of the head, made of massive oak timbers. Just inside the bow the team in Lot 32 was uncovering parts of the upper or weather deck, which had collapsed into the hull. Farther aft, in the ten-by-ten-foot reconnaissance pit we had initially excavated, an archaeologist was using water from a garden hose to clean a large section of the lower deck and the main hatch for a photography session. It was a scene of intense energy, as crew members with assigned tasks moved throughout the site digging, recording, packaging artifacts, and moving timbers.

The archaeologists recorded and kept obvious "diagnostic" artifacts within each level of fill. As they dug, they shoveled the fill into the five-gallon pickle buckets, retaining every tenth bucket of fill for sample testing. A separate team washed the samples for small artifact retrieval and conducted "float tests" of the soil to retrieve seeds and other floating remains. We judged that only the bottom layer of fill and anything between the hull's ceiling planking and outer planking might be originally from the ship. After the fieldwork, all that material was carefully screened for artifacts. Because of time and funding constraints we were forced to discard the fill that had not been saved for sample testing and was not part of the original ship's ballast.

Is it Murphy's Law that fieldwork never proceeds as planned? Digging, recording, and preserving timbers progressed, sometimes smoothly and other times at a snail's pace. We combated the constant seepage of groundwater and tried to anticipate what we were to encounter next in the site. With effort we did our best to contend with distractions of the city bustling around the block, the seemingly endless poor weather, and the deafening noise of construction work near our excavation.

We had our share of near disasters. While we excavated, preliminary construction crews began to work on the west side of the block and occasionally encroached into our work area. On a particularly bad afternoon in the second week a construction carpentry crew dropped a ten-foot-long two-by-four board that just missed two women working fifteen feet below. When Sheli insisted that the carpentry crew stop the work above our people, they professed to speak no English. They eventually relocated when threatened in several languages, but we discovered that they had also removed some shoring braces that kept the eastern mud walls from sliding down upon our team. When the incident was brought to his attention, the construction manager made sure that those workers did not come onto the site for the rest of our excavation.

On the very same day we had a rash of small accidents. My field notes record: "David Babson hit right thumb. Sarah [Keyishian] cut her hand. Philip [Perazio] got dirt in his eye and went to the hospital." Quentin pointed out that the crew was probably too tired, so we shortened the next day.

At quitting time late that afternoon, as I dropped the site baseline (see glossary) for the night, I discovered that a pile driver crew had untied the baseline during our lunch break and had retied it incorrectly without informing us. All the measurements for the

The excavation teams often worked deep in mud. This is the central cargo hold, looking forward, showing a portion of the collapsed lower deck. The noise from water pumps, backhoes, a large excavator, and a pile driver was often so loud that we needed to use two-way radios to talk, even when only fifteen feet apart. *Photo by Robert Adams, courtesy of the Mariners' Museum.*

afternoon were therefore inaccurate. Since the teams removed artifacts and dismantled parts of the ship after measuring and sketching them, we could not retake many of the measurements after I discovered the problem. I would need to correct all of them as best I could using field sketches, photographs, and mathematics after we left the field.

On other days, seemingly disastrous situations were quickly defused by the crew. On two separate occasions we were picketed by minority labor coalitions. They thought we were a construction crew with few minority workers. When members of the crew informed them that we were only a temporary archaeology crew, making approximately half the wages of a union day laborer in New York, they left us alone. Late one day a Molotov cocktail arced through the air, just missing the construction company's utility trailer, followed by a street gang running through an open gate waving clubs and chains. But no sooner had they entered the site than a large number of our mud-covered team came flying up out of the ship with shovels to meet them on their flank. In front of the gang, two construction workers jumped off their machines and advanced with heavy tools in their hands. The street gang quickly retreated before there was any physical contact. We never knew if the attack was random or aimed at the site for some reason, but security was increased, including a guard making sure that the vehicle gate was closed after each truck passed through.

The ship was not uniformly preserved, so that as one team made great progress in the aft end of the cargo hold, the team just forward of them found the upper deck had collapsed onto the lower deck long before, forcing them to record and extricate the deck pieces ever more carefully. As we excavated deeper we had to go far below the water level. Each day we used three or four portable pumps to lower the water, with the hull still doing a fair job of keeping water out of the hold after 230 years. If we kept the ship dry through February the fragile old wood would be destroyed by drying and freezing. We therefore shut the pumps down at night to allow the ship to refill with water, and an early morning team started the pumps before the full crew arrived.

Every morning we had more water to pump out of the hull as our teams excavated deeper into it. The hull at the stern was shallow, so when they finished recording it, that team was shifted to the main cargo hold, where the hull was deeper and there was much more to dig and record. As the teams removed soil from the site into the five-gallon pails, they then emptied these into hundred-gallon steel buckets. The backhoe operators hoisted the steel buckets out of the hull with a hook and cable and dumped the dirt at a designated spot, far away from the ship. When the excavators were too deep in the hold for the backhoe to operate safely, one member of the team hauled each plastic pail up a twelve-foot wooden slide with a snap-line and emptied the soil into the steel buckets.

A stench of river silt and clay was our constant companion, especially within the hull. The noise on the site was deafening and constant. Typically, we were running four gas-driven pumps and two backhoes. The Fuller Company was already working in the rest of the city block with a large excavator and driving sixty-foot steel piles with a pile driver, sometimes only fifty feet from the ship. Most of the time we could not hear each other, even when yelling from fifteen feet away. We purchased earplugs for the entire crew and six two-way radios for the supervisors and equipment operators. Although radios likely saved us a day's time over the course of the month, major snowstorms forced two days of rest.

Most of the crew lived nearby, commuting each day on the subway. However the nautical archaeology crew members were from out of state. We stayed at the Howard Johnson Hotel, Midtown, and generally commuted by subway. Each morning we would meet at a health bar near the site for breakfast with team supervisors Burt and Jay to discuss plans for the day. Around noon each day we broke to have lunch with the crew at one of the few nearby restaurants that would serve people who left a trail of mud behind. Because of this problem, toward the end of the project HRO provided catered hot lunches near the site for the crew. Our return commute most days was different from our morning rides downtown. Even during the afternoon rush hour we were given plenty of space on the subway trains as frozen mud dripped off our foul weather gear and helmets—we were probably mistaken for sewer workers. Back at the hotel we would try to get as much mud off our clothes as possible and out of our pores, then eat at a different midtown restaurant each night. Three times we were able to obtain half-price tickets to Broadway shows that were playing within an easy walk from the hotel; but we were usually much too tired to do anything after dinner except write in our project journals. This was our daily routine through most of the month as we worked at least six days each week.

To facilitate recording the site in the time allotted, rather than using the common land archaeology techniques of capturing the X, Y, and Z (east, north, and down) coordinates rectilinearly, we turned to underwater techniques that we had developed to capture best a ship's curvilinear hull. Quentin constructed a number of five-by-five-foot grids over each excavation unit. The crews used three measuring tapes attached to specific corners on the grids to record each location on the site. Since the positions of the points on the grid were known, and only one mathematical solution existed for each set of three distances below the grid, the position of each point could be calculated later.

With hundreds of decisions to make during a site investigation, some will prove to be incorrect. Using the trilateration measuring system was one of the three major mistakes we made during the fieldwork that would haunt me for many years. In hindsight, it might have been better to let the experienced crew use the familiar rectilinear measuring method because they would have been more likely to spot measuring errors as they recorded them if they used a familiar method. It also took longer than expected to train them in the new method, and it took time to construct the needed measuring grids and align them each day.

The second mistake of significance was not replacing the site plan illustrator when he left. During an excavation one person is assigned to keep a running map or plan of the site, updating it daily with recorded data to catch errors in a timely manner and to use to update planning. We were using the illustrator who had worked for Joan Geismar during the terrestrial excavation in the block, but when he had to leave, we decided not to replace him. No one remembers why we made that decision.

Our third and most important error was not photocopying our notes on a daily basis. Accustomed to working off islands, boats, and other places not close to offices, our standard method was to take particular care of our waterproof, tear-resistant notebooks and forms, then copy them at the end of a field season. It was 1982, before portable copiers and scanners. However, here we were in New York City, surrounded by thousands of offices and staying at a hotel. We had the resources to have everything photocopied each evening, but fatigue can mar one's judgment. So focused were we on completing a precision excavation in a short time, even in the poor weather, that we made some fateful mistakes.

As we descended deeper into the hull, under a layer of dirt and refuse in the midship area we found much of the upper or weather deck. It was collapsed into the ship but was otherwise fairly intact, including a cargo hatchway. Remnants of a small campfire were also on this deck. Below the upper deck we excavated through three feet of river silt and dirt and came upon the lower deck. Throughout most of the ship we found the complete lower deck, which would have been just above the waterline, collapsed into the ship. It looked as if during the eighteenth century, aft of the mainmast, workers had removed the deck planks from the remaining deck beams. Below the lower deck, in the ship's cargo hold, we excavated through another layer of dredged river silt and several layers of exotic material such as black volcanic sand, coral, and flint that seemed to be excess ballast from other ships.

During this process we were always conscious of being in an ever-deepening hole, many feet below street level. I reminded the supervisors that the ship was surrounded by water-saturated mud that pressed in against the hull; along with everything else, they needed to keep an eye on the ship timbers around us. One night in the third week the old foundation wall across the hull in the cargo hold collapsed. Luckily no one was around when it happened, but the next morning we were faced with tons of debris to remove. The incident's silver lining was that we then had the entire length of the cargo hold to study. After the wall's collapse the SSI safety engineer had us survey every day the relative height of the remaining building walls to make sure they were not slumping. Another day toward the end of February three breast hooks (massive timbers on the inside of the bow) collapsed down around two archaeologists recording in the bow, narrowly missing each of them. While wooden trunnels held almost all of the ship tightly together, the thick iron fasteners for the breast hooks had corroded and become too weak to hold the heavy timbers from being shaken free by the nearby pile driver.

At each layer of fill and each deck the archaeology teams measured, mapped, and photographed their area. They recorded, labeled, and recovered *diagnostics*—artifacts that would be particularly helpful for analysis. In addition, key ship timbers were recorded in place and then sent to the wood recording team on the surface, who then also documented the timber with measurements, drawings, and photography.

At times during the month several nautical

The wood recording team, ankle-deep in freezing mud throughout February, measured, drew, photographed, and cataloged every diagnostic timber or plank sent up by the excavation archaeologists. *Photo by Robert Adams, courtesy of the Mariners' Museum.*

An archaeologist shoveling another ship's excess ballast used to fill the hull near the mainmast step. This layer consisted of coral sand with small and large pieces of brain coral. *Photo by Robert Adams, courtesy of the Mariners' Museum.*

An archaeologist hoses away the last bits of coral sand in the main cargo hold to ready the ship's floor for photographic recording. *Photo by Robert Adams, courtesy of the Mariners' Museum.*

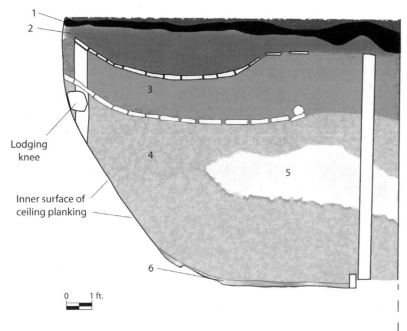

Stratigraphy of the north face of the main cargo hold, showing the collapsed upper and lower decks, the top of a frame and cross section of a lodging knee on the left, and a vertical stanchion on the right. *From a field illustration by B. Herbert.*

Lodging knee

Inner surface of ceiling planking

0 ___ 1 ft.

approximate centerline

1. Black sandy soil. 2. Brown gray sandy soil 3. Gray sandy clay with stones and flint. 4. Gray sandy silt with pebbles and large rocks 5. White sand with crushed shell and coral. 6. Tan yellow silt with crushed shell and coral.

archaeologists visited us at the site and helped with advice and physical work in the dirt. Gordon Watts, from North Carolina, and John Broadwater, from Virginia, each visited for a few days, among other things tunneling east toward the street to find the sternpost at the ship's center. J. Richard Steffy, one of our mentors from Texas A&M and the Institute of Nautical Archaeology, flew up for two days to inspect the ship and advise us, just as Peter Throckmorton arrived from Maine to do the same. Their observations and our discussions with them helped us better understand some features and further underlined to us the site's significance. Faith and Peter Hentschel, from the Institute of Nautical Archaeology, arrived to help with advice and toil.

As our month's work was coming to an end, the future of the ship's remains was still in question. The hull could not stay in place because the new office building was to be supported by more than three hundred steel piles, and they could not be driven through the ship because its oak timbers remained too tough to penetrate. We were carefully documenting the dimensions and shapes of every timber, so that we could draw up and model the ship in the future. But future researchers and the public would be deprived of an important piece of American history if the ship were totally destroyed or removed and left to deteriorate, which would happen in a few months if the timbers

were left untreated. We could remove the whole hull, but the cost of conserving that much wood was an estimated three million dollars in 1982. Building a controlled-environment museum to house it in lower Manhattan and supporting continued maintenance would amount to many more millions of dollars.

After discussions among the various parties and with outside consultants from the United States and Canada, the New York City Landmarks Preservation Commission and HRO came to an agreement: the bow qualified as such an important treasure that it had to be saved. However, after carefully studying it we were to abandon the rest of the ship. Howard Ronson offered to underwrite the conservation of the bow.

Two days later John Sands, director of collections at the Mariners' Museum in Newport News, Virginia, stopped in for a visit. As I led him through the ship remains he inspected the timbers and became even more interested when it seemed to him that most of the ship's heavy timbers were made of live oak (*Quercus virginiana*, a southern North American species), and the decks were mostly southern pine. We discussed the possibility that it had been built in the Chesapeake to carry tobacco to the British Isles. A few days later he called to advise that if no museum in New York wanted the bow, the Mariners' Museum might like it for their planned new Chesapeake exhibit wing.

Removing ceiling planks from the midships area. *Photo by Robert Adams, courtesy of the Mariners' Museum.*

Sheli Smith (left), Warren Riess (center), and Eugene Boesch plan the dismantling of the bow to remove it for preservation while a steam pile driver shakes the earth 20 feet away. *Photo by Robert Adams, courtesy of the Mariners' Museum.*

By the end of February each team had reached the bottom of the ship. At last we were standing on the hull's inner planks, known as the ceiling planks. It was an extraordinary experience to step back in time and walk around in an early eighteenth-century ship, but we had to concentrate on the job at hand to finish documenting the site before the deadline.

To develop a visual representation of the shape of the hull in order to compare this ship to others found in archives or archaeology sites, we needed to measure the outside of the ship's frames. We therefore took off each of the two-inch thick ceiling planks that covered the frames and removed the silt lodged between the frames. During the last days, when the massive curved frames were exposed and cleaned, Sheli and her team recorded the ship's shape at fourteen stations by erecting a pole with a large protractor over each desired frame and measuring the angle and distance to several points along the outside edge of the frame. They chose data points at each outer planking edge in order to record the outer planks' widths in the same task.

In addition to the team excavating, taking thousands of measurements, and making sketches and notes, Bob Adams took approximately a thousand photographs of the ship remains during various phases of the excavation. HRO also hired Sam Low, a renowned documentary producer, to record the excavation process with professional-quality film footage.

Until February 27 knowledge of the ship had not been made public. HRO had surrounded the site with a twelve-foot plywood fence with no peep holes, and all members of the archaeology and construction crews were constantly reminded to keep the nature of the site quiet. Any possible site vandals or press had the potential to destroy information and slow us down. Yet, it was such a unique site that Mayor Ed Koch wanted the

A backhoe operator raises one of the heavy oak breasthooks out of the bow in order to submerge it in the holding pool. *Photo by Robert Adams, courtesy of the Mariners' Museum.*

On February 28, people lined up outside the site for four blocks to have a chance to see the ship while we continued to excavate and record its details. *Photo by Robert Adams, courtesy of the Mariners' Museum.*

public to see it. In late February, as we neared the end of our work, Fuller Construction built a walkway above us for a major opening. By Saturday, February 27, our team had excavated most of the ship as the mayor and the press came to view, videotape, and write about the site. The next day, possibly the only sunny day of February, nearly twelve thousand interested viewers queued for an hour and a half along four city blocks to get a close look at the ship while we continued working below.

By March 2, our excavation teams had finished their work, carefully recording and removing the bottom layer of ballast sand and artifacts, removing the ceiling planking, and washing down the ship's timbers.

Sheli's five-person hull-recording team marked, photographed, measured, and drew the ship's ceiling planking, frames, and lines. Recording the hull during those last two days was a difficult task. Rain and freezing rain made the site more dangerous, complicated sketching and recording, and rendered photography near to impossible. But the team persevered, knowing there was much to record and save before the contractors would destroy the site at 7:00 a.m. on March 4, only two days away.

During the last two days we placed Eugene Boesch and Abby Jaroslow in charge of a small team to remove the bow. Eugene had been working in the bow all month and clearly understood the intricacies of its structure better than anyone. Abby had spent some time as a construction rigger. Dismantling the bow piece by piece, rather than removing it whole, was the best way to proceed. This method is usually better for the hull analysis, because we would be able to study every facet of each timber, and is better for the eventual conservation of the timbers, because each timber could be treated individually. As Eugene guided the

Eugene Boesch taking apart the bow, using softwood wedges and a mallet. Any iron fastenings had corroded to a soft, black goo, but wooden trunnels still held most of the ship together. *Photo by Robert Adams, courtesy of the Mariners' Museum.*

Abby Jaroslow gently removed each bow timber, here a cheek outside the bow, by expertly strapping it and hand signaling the backhoe operator. *Photo by Robert Adams, courtesy of the Mariners' Museum*

Minutes after we had finished, a large excavator began to remove the hull because the piles to be used to support the new building could not be driven through the ship's oak timbers. The excavator operator was careful to put aside any timber when Sheli Smith radioed him that there was something we could not see during the archaeological excavation. *Photo by Robert Adams, courtesy of the Mariners' Museum*

dismantling by wedging off each timber, Abby and her helpers quickly slipped nylon lifting straps on it and signaled the backhoe/crane operator for removal.

The temperature remained above freezing on that penultimate night, so we pumped the site dry through the night to get a quick start in the morning. While Sheli rested to be at the site early the next morning, Dick Swete and I remained and took turns throughout

the night monitoring and adding fuel to the pumps. Dick had been through graduate school with Sheli and me, and together we had spent summers searching for and studying ships underwater. That night the two of us climbed down a ladder into the hull and took a last long look at the ship while a cold drizzle fell and the beating of the pumps' engines drowned out the sounds of the city. Silently, each alone in our thoughts, we had the privilege of walking through the cargo hold of an early eighteenth-century merchant ship; a vessel that had not seen the light of day in more than two hundred years. I wondered if we would ever find the ship's identity and history. Perhaps not, but I was determined to try.

As we looked up the sides of the ship in the dim light we smiled with wonder and a little pride at the progress the team had made in the past thirty days. In some places we were twenty-three feet below the street level. The hard work, the strength of the ship's timbers, and the grace of its shape had bonded the whole team to one another and to the ship for life. And yet we knew it would be coming apart soon. Dick and I hardly spoke a word to each other as we each privately envisioned the people who had built and manned this ship more than two centuries earlier, and as we contemplated the next and last twenty-four hours of the excavation.

In the morning of the last full day the bow team began working steadily to dismantle the bow, taking turns with volunteers from the other lots. Everyone else finished taking samples, recording data, and removing field equipment from the ship. When night came we continued in an eerily lit atmosphere created by rented floodlights and near-freezing rain. Working from the bow aft, the mud-covered bow team systematically wedged off one timber after another while the backhoe operators relocated each piece from the ship to a water-filled holding pool. Everyone was beyond tired. Through the night each of us in turn would give up, but rally again, convinced by the others to continue—we *could* finish in time to save the bow. We had planned to remove the first twenty-five feet of the bow, but in the dark early morning hours, after the first

eighteen feet were removed, the mud walls on either side of the crew began to slump a little. It was a dangerous situation to which I reacted with: "Everyone out of the pool!"

As the sun rose at dawn, an hour before our deadline, only the ship's fourteen-foot stem remained, too heavy for our backhoes to lift. The construction crew brought over their massive excavator, shackled the lifting straps to its bucket, and gently lifted the stem out of the mud and into the holding pool. We all silently watched as the excavator operator then turned his machine on the remainder of the hull, tearing the timbers apart and loading them onto a squadron of waiting dump trucks, to be used for land fill on Staten Island.

I looked at the mud-spattered faces of the crew. The entire team was spent. We had worked for twenty-eight of the last thirty-one days, including all of the last ten days and all of the last twenty-four hours, through mostly foul weather and some highly stressful moments. However, the first stage of our mission was accomplished—individuals and strangers to one another had coalesced to form a team and unite our efforts to complete the fieldwork successfully. We learned from one another and made long-term professional and personal friends. Two couples who met on the dig eventually married. On the night of March 4, Howard Ronson threw a large party for the crew to celebrate a job well done. It was the first time many of us had seen one another scrubbed and sporting clothes that did not include a hard hat, winter work coat, rain pants, and boots. That evening we realized this most intense excavation was over. Years of preservation, analysis, and interpretation were about to begin.

Preservation for the Future

CONSERVING ARTIFACTS involves a delicate chemical balance. Preserving artifacts that have been submerged in water for centuries is a complex endeavor, requiring the time of skilled conservators and a substantial investment of physical and financial resources. Yet preserving the ship's bow timbers and the artifacts found in the ship would allow us to learn from them in the 1980s and to learn more in the future. Archaeologists have to keep in mind that technology and analytical techniques improve quickly, so that scientists even in the near future are often able to find information from the artifacts that we cannot find today. While archaeologists and historians could study the site's material as a related collection for decades, if not centuries, it was also important to consider the scientific information, beyond the fields of archaeology and history, that could be gleaned from the collection. For example, biologists can investigate the species of eighteenth-century plants and animals found between and within the ship timbers. Should the collection be exhibited, preserving it would also allow public access and help bring the past alive for museum visitors. It was fortunate for everyone that HRO understood this and accepted the responsibility to expend the resources necessary to conserve as much of the material as possible.

As we found them, artifacts uncovered within the ship were in a precarious state. Organic, metal, ceramic, and glass materials are all very unstable after being soaked in groundwater for long periods of time. Proper first aid in the field, careful conservation processes in the laboratory, and stable environments for storage and exhibition are all necessary to preserve artifacts from a wet site.

The artifacts in the Ronson ship had been soaked for 230 years in water and mud. Underwater, some matter leached out of most of the artifacts, while dissolved salts, mostly iron and chloride compounds, seeped into the cells of the organic material and between the structural layers of ceramic, glass, and metal artifacts. Dissolved salts are a time bomb for the destruction of artifacts. If the artifacts are dried with the salts still in them, salts will crystallize throughout the material's structure. Since salt crystals absorb and release water from the air, if the humidity rises and falls after drying, the crystals will grow and contract repeatedly. This process would destroy the already weakened cell walls of organic material and exfoliate any glass and glazed pottery. Metal artifacts have the added misfortune of being corroded by the chemical action of wet salts on their surfaces and within their structure, while degrading iron contributes to the degradation of wood in several ways.

Organics on the site, mostly wood, leather, and bone, were also subject to attack from bacteria and fungi. Shortly after being buried in the 1700s, the artifacts and mud that surrounded them became an anaerobic environment, where no oxygen could support most organic-eating microorganisms. Thus the material survived for more than two hundred years in place, but it could not last for more than a few days if removed without proper care. As soon as we removed the mud surrounding the artifacts, organic materials were open to attack from microbes, as well as subjected to freezing and drying, even while barely strong enough to support themselves. We administered first aid to them after recording and removal, mostly by keeping the hundreds of small and large objects submerged in water.

While we excavated, it was critical to keep the site wet by letting the groundwater flood the hull each night, and on some days we kept large ship timbers damp by covering the wood with burlap and plastic or salt hay and spraying it with water. Since it was a particularly wet February, there was usually more of a problem keeping the staff dry than keeping the wood saturated. To establish a holding pool for removed ship timbers, one of the backhoe operators dug out a small building basement at the north end of the block. We lined it with plastic and filled it with water from a fire hydrant. Besides keeping the timbers wet, the pool allowed us to begin the process of removing the surface mud and leaching out salts from the wood. We kept the small artifacts in buckets of water.

At first we planned to keep only diagnostic timbers from the ship, such as particular knees and sample beams, planks, futtocks, and trunnels (dowels). Once the decision was made to save the bow, we knew we would have many tons of large timbers and fragile planks to transport and conserve. For transportation we rented a "rollaway," a 20 x 8 x 8-foot trash container often seen at construction sites. It was rolled off a large truck, to be left at the site for the days we needed it, and later rolled back onto a truck for transportation. Our crew lined the rollaway with two layers of plastic and ran water into it with a hose. When leaks proved too many to contain the water, we replaced the regular garden hoses with perforated soaker hose. In this manner, water sprinkled or dripped on the burlap-wrapped wood day and night. Shortly after the excavation we moved the loaded container to a holding site at Floyd Bennett Field on Staten Island while a new conservation laboratory was prepared. During the next four months the container sat in a hanger with a small fire hose continually adding water to keep the timbers submerged.

Finding a laboratory on the East Coast that could handle such a large quantity of wood was impossible at the time. Soil Systems therefore decided to establish their own in Groton, Massachusetts, near their northeast regional office directed by Michael Roberts. He hired Conservator Betty Seifert, leased a barn, and began to convert it into a wet-artifact conservation laboratory. Betty had been a conservator at the Maine State Museum, where she worked for six years on the collection of artifacts from the underwater excavation of the Revolutionary War Privateer *Defence*.

When Betty had the laboratory ready for the timbers, Sheli returned to Manhattan to accompany the wood on its two-hundred-mile trip to Groton. After a harrowing night in New York and a twelve-hour drive including dodging weight limit inspections, Sheli, the truck driver, and the ship's bow finally reached the conservation laboratory at 3:00 p.m.

We had a crew of archaeologists, conservators, and four extra-large, extra-strong hired helpers ready when the truck arrived. With a rented forklift and much physical labor, each piece of wood was carefully lifted out of the container and immersed in new tanks filled with well water.

As soon as the truck left, Betty and her staff began the planned conservation process, which included cleaning, washing, saturation with polyethylene glycol (PEG), and drying. They could gently lift, move, and lower the heavy oak with straps and a chain hoist that rolled on a system of rails hanging from the laboratory ceiling. The team cleaned the mud-encrusted timbers with water hoses, soft brushes, and dental picks, gently removing the mud and iron deposits from the wood. If left, the iron deposits, mostly eighteenth-century nails that had oxidized into a soft black goop, would further harm the wood and would react chemically with some of the preservatives to be used later. This is a time-consuming process, sometimes taking a day or more for a large timber. Once they completed the physical cleaning, the conservators placed each timber in fresh water to begin leaching out the many salt compounds that had dissolved into the wood.

At the end of six months of continually flushing with water, the conservators immersed the pieces in a weak (3 percent) solution of hydrochloric acid for two days. The acid would dissolve the remaining iron residue. Then they hoisted the timbers out of the acid and into pools of more fresh water to purge them of the acid, dissolved iron, and other salts. For the next three months the staff routinely changed the water in the pools to finish the washing process.

Once the wood was clear of harmful salts and iron, the laboratory staff and volunteers began adding polyethylene glycol to the pools of water and wood. PEG is a synthetic water-soluble wax used for many things, including to treat green wood, coat fruit for preservation, give "body" to lipstick, and as a mild laxative. Saturating waterlogged wood with PEG has become one of the standard conservation practices. The wax penetrates into and around weakened cell walls, helping prevent the wood from collapsing when it is eventually dried.

During the next six months Betty gradually increased the percentage of PEG to water from zero to 25 percent. If one did not change the solution slowly, one might damage the wood cells with chemical shock. The timbers soaked in the PEG bath for the next two years, slowly absorbing the wax into their cells. Structural analysis at the University of Maine confirmed that while some of the wood was quite degraded, other wood was still quite sound and dense. We expected the PEG to penetrate only about one inch into the sound wood after thirty months.

With the large timbers securely submerged in their long-term PEG bath, Betty and her staff turned their attention to the small artifacts recovered from the site. The original research plan for the 175 Water Street block did not call for a complete conservation treatment of all 300,000 artifacts found on the block. In the initial plan they were to be washed, analyzed, and safely stored. The majority would survive for years with that limited treatment, but the particularly sensitive artifacts, such as those made of organics, glass, and most metals, would be lost to degradation soon after analysis. When the ship was found and excavated, some 5,000 more artifacts were recovered. They were mostly ceramic sherds, used pieces of leather, and other typical eighteenth-century refuse. Though we had no budget to conserve anything from the ship completely except the hull timbers, Betty, Sheli, and Lisa Goldberg surveyed the 5,000 artifacts, selecting and saving almost 300 important diagnostic artifacts found in the ship. The rest were left to be washed and dried.

Betty took the selected artifacts to the laboratory and dedicated her own time to work on them. Among the finds she conserved from the ship site were mid-1700s whole shoes and shoe parts, metal buckles, a mechanical pencil, buttons, clay pipe fragments, musket balls, and a whole spirits bottle. There were also a few ship artifacts, such as belaying pins, many trunnels, a deck brush, and a bucket and brush for tarring the vessel's rigging. She treated the leather and wood artifacts much as she did the bow timbers: by cleaning, recording, washing, and saturating them with PEG.

Glass and glazed ceramics need to be treated differently. When old glass is submerged for many years, the lime between the layers of glass is dissolved and it migrates out of the object. It is replaced by other compounds in the water, such as chloride salts. If the glass is dried without treatment the salts will crystallize within the layers of glass. As the humidity in storage rises and drops, the salt crystals will grow and shrink with absorbed water. When that happens the salt crystals break the layers of glass and the object will slowly fragment, usually seen as continuous flaking of the outer layer.

Another problem exists with waterlogged glass. If one submerges the glass object immediately into fresh water the osmotic pressure of dissolved salts within the layer of glass will push out toward the fresh water. Flaking then occurs underwater in the laboratory. To overcome these problems the conservation staff left the artifacts in the New York groundwater in which they were transported. Very slowly, over a one-year period, they lowered the salt content in the water by periodically taking out a little of the old water and replacing it with deionized water. Weekly they monitored the progress of the treatment by measuring the amount of salts leached into the water bath with electronic instruments. When all the salts had left the glass, the conservators gradually dried each artifact and applied a protective acrylic coating (Acryloid B-72). Most of the glazed ceramics were given the same treatment as glass because fired glaze is actually glass.

The other major category of artifact composition was metal. Most of the metal objects were in a very weak condition because they were oxidized and saturated with water-borne salts. Technicians cleaned each object, bathed it in deionized water to remove any salts, and subjected it to electrolytic reduction. In this practice, the object was attached to the negative lead from a weak direct current power source. It was then immersed in a bath of sodium hydroxide, which also contained a positive electrical lead. Very slowly the electric charge freed the metal atoms from any attached nonmetals, such as oxygen or chlorine. In this manner electrolytic reduction altered the objects' chemistry back a little toward their original all-metal composition to stabilize the metal artifacts. We found it especially satisfying to see small objects such as buttons transform from a corroded green mass to pleasingly detailed designs in brass.

In two years' time PEG had penetrated into the hull timbers to various depths, depending on the wood's density. Initial plans called for the wood to be freeze-dried at this point, but tests made on extra timbers, saved from the site for this purpose, proved troublesome. A nearby commercial aerospace testing facility had a large chamber for testing space vehicles. The chamber was large enough to drive a truck into it, its temperature could be lowered to below what was needed for freeze-drying, and it could sustain a near perfect vacuum. This should allow the conservators to freeze-dry all of the heavy timbers in one operation. But when they tried some of the test timbers in the chamber, its vacuum pump broke. The system was made to evacuate normal air from the chamber, not the quantity of water vapor coming out of the waterlogged timbers. Ice formed inside the vacuum pump, ruining it. Replacing the pump was an expensive ordeal. Replacing it with a system that could handle the water vapor that would come out of the bow timbers was beyond the budget of anyone involved. Two commercial freeze-drying businesses were located, but the costs of transporting the timbers and processing them at either facility also were prohibitive.

While Betty struggled with the conservation problems, others worked to find the best home for the ship's bow and artifacts. Howard Ronson offered to donate the collection to the museum best able to preserve and exhibit it. At first, New York seemed a logical place for the collection to remain. Yet to exhibit the collection would require a large area with at least twenty-foot ceilings and sophisticated environmental controls. Caring for the collection, especially the bow, involved a long-term commitment of space, staff, and funds. Even when Mayor Koch pledged $50,000 of New York City municipal funds, a coalition within New York could not raise the necessary resources to curate the collection properly.

A timely offer arrived when the Mariners' Museum in Newport News, Virginia, officially reiterated their desire to acquire the collection to exhibit in their planned Chesapeake exhibit. The Mariners' Museum is the largest indoor maritime museum in the Americas and sits in the middle of its own 800-acre park, which includes a 300-acre lake. The museum had the space, the professional staff, and other resources necessary to curate the bow and artifacts properly. Following months of discussions of various options, all parties, including New York officials, agreed that the Mariners' Museum should become the final home for the Ronson ship collection. Consequently, at about the same time as the wood was due to come out of the PEG pools, HRO donated the Ronson ship collection to the Mariners' Museum.

After the freeze-drying experience, the museum staff and Betty decided to use a controlled drying process for the timbers that Steve Brooke, Ken Morris,

and she had developed at the Maine State Museum for their waterlogged wood. The timbers would be placed on racks in a room where technicians would drop the relative humidity slowly from 98 to 55 percent in three years. While the wood dried, conservators would keep a coat of PEG 1450 solution (made of large PEG molecules) on its surface. Ideally the PEG 1450 would be sucked into the wood as the water came out. Given the large size of the PEG 1450 molecules, penetration into the wood would be shallow. It dries to the consistency of candle wax, so it would keep the earlier liquid PEG in the wood while providing a fairly hard surface for the wood when it dried. Tests conducted at the Groton laboratory on extra pieces of the Ronson ship had shown that this process would produce satisfactory results. Its disadvantages were that it required more time, a large sealed room, and much more labor and PEG than the freeze-drying method.

In May 1985, three years after the Manhattan excavation, a refrigerated eighteen-wheel truck backed up to the Groton laboratory to transport the collection to Newport News. We hoisted each ship timber out of its PEG pool, applied PEG on each surface with whitewash brushes, and made one large layer of wood within the truck's trailer. Handling the large, curved, heavy pieces that weighed over a hundred pounds was particularly awkward and dangerous once they were coated with the slippery PEG. The smaller wrapped and boxed artifacts made the trip to Virginia in a smaller truck.

In Newport News, the Mariners' Museum staff had prepared a room for the ship's larger timbers. A large, easily accessed storage room in the basement seemed the ideal location for the next phase of preservation. All four walls, the ceiling, and floor were made of concrete or concrete block, which would act as a humidity sink, readily absorbing or releasing large quantities of moisture, and thereby maintaining a relatively constant humidity within the room. The museum staff placed the large timbers in the storage room, thinner planking in a pool of PEG solution, and the already conserved and dried smaller artifacts in one of the museum's environmentally controlled storage areas.

As the Ronson ship collection was being secured at the Mariners' Museum, Sheli and I were packing our bags for a three-month stay in Virginia that eventually extended to three years. I worked at the museum to help organize the collection and continue the conservation treatments, and I ultimately became a curator there. Sheli worked nearby at the excavation of a Revolutionary War shipwreck site in Yorktown, Virginia. Her proximity enabled her to make regular trips to Newport News to lend assistance with the curation needs of the collection. She organized and cataloged the small artifacts, leading a team of gray-smocked volunteers called the "gray ladies" until they appropriately renamed themselves the "caged ladies," as every Wednesday afternoon was spent in a caged security area.

Once a week the museum's "slop team"—four other staff members and I dressed in green coveralls, rubber gloves, and filtered breathing masks—descended from our pristine, environmentally controlled collections department into the basement room that held the ship's 126 heavy bow timbers. That first summer, with the relative humidity at 97 percent and the temperature averaging 76° F, it was essential to add a biodegradable biocide to the PEG solution in order to retard any fungus growth. The slop team brushed this syrupy solution onto all four surfaces of each timber, turning the slippery wood as needed.

A museum technician spreads a thick layer of polyethylene glycol (PEG) on the surface of the ship's stem as it slowly dries in the Mariner's Museum's basement. *Photo by Gregg Vick, courtesy of the Mariners' Museum.*

During the next thirty-six months we lowered the relative humidity an average of 1 percent each month, except once when the wood seemed to overreact to a slight change. In that situation we kept the moisture content of the air steady for four months while the wood slowly expelled its excess water. Betty Seifert came to the museum every six months to inspect the wood. After checking each piece, taking small core samples, and probing, she adjusted our treatment schedule to fit the wood's needs better. As time progressed we reduced the frequency of the PEG applications and eventually stopped altogether when the wood had absorbed as much as it could.

The shape of most of the timbers remained unchanged, with almost no shrinkage in their outer dimensions. However, a certain amount of cell collapse was inevitable, causing some large and many small checks in the wood. During the slow-drying process, as the first checks opened, we were surprised to find dirt in many of them. Then we realized that the cracks were old and had existed in the timbers when the ship was an active, sea-going vessel. All wooden vessels have checks throughout their timbers. When the New York colonists buried the ship, dirt lodged in the checks, and then, buried below the water level, the wood swelled and its checks closed. As the checks reopened in the drying process, they revealed the trapped dirt.

By January 1988, almost three years after the timbers arrived in Virginia, we had lowered the moisture in the air around the bow timbers to 55 percent relative humidity, and the wood appeared to be in great shape. The surfaces were relatively hard, mostly caused by the consistency of dry PEG 1450, and they retained much of their original detail. Carved numbers and tool marks made by the shipbuilders more than 250 years before were evident on the timbers. For extra protection during storage, we applied a heavy coat of PEG that in the future could easily be removed with warmth and rags.

When we started the conservation treatment Betty estimated that if the weak wood were only slow-dried, without PEG, approximately half of the timbers would survive as found, and half would fall apart or twist and shrink out of shape. She argued that if we used the best treatment possible at the time (which we did), we might lose 5 to 10 percent of the pieces. Since we had carefully recorded each of the bow pieces, we would be able to recreate any damaged pieces when we reconstructed the bow. Over time, none of the pieces fell apart, and only six of the 450 pieces twisted out of shape—less than a 2 percent loss.

Today, in the spring of 2014, all the bow timbers and artifacts are stabilized and stored with care at the Mariners' Museum. Though the surface of the wood is hard and covered by a thick layer of white PEG, the insides of the heavy timbers, where the wax could not penetrate, is still fragile. Many of the artifacts will always be sensitive to ultraviolet light and changes in humidity, especially those artifacts containing PEG. The artifacts also pose a threat to other artifacts in a museum's collection. Old wood and other organics, even when treated with PEG, give off trace amounts of sulfur to the air. Although this is no problem to people, long-term contact with sulfur in the air can cause surface problems for paintings, photographs, and artifacts with silver surfaces.

The museum staff is therefore careful to keep the Ronson ship artifacts stored on solid supports in separate areas that have a steady 55 percent relative humidity and no ultraviolet light. The same will have to be true if the ship and artifacts are exhibited. The environment in the exhibit hall will have to be carefully controlled, and the air needs to be kept separate from that of the rest of the museum's buildings. This can be accomplished with filters or by having other museum air pressure-vented into the ship exhibit area and then outside.

Considering the harsh conditions the artifacts endured under the waterfront and buildings for two and a half centuries, they are quite well preserved. They should survive many centuries in the Mariners' Museum's environmentally controlled storage facilities or exhibit halls. A commitment by so many dedicated people to provide the resources, careful first aid at the HRO site in Manhattan, individual professional treatment at the SSI conservation laboratory, and thorough treatment and storage by the staff of the Mariners' Museum all contributed to preserve this unique eighteenth-century collection.

CHAPTER FIVE

A Close Look at the Ship

DURING THE SITE EXCAVATION, the team diligently observed details about the ship and recorded everything possible for future study; however, there was not much time during fieldwork to analyze what we saw. Some of our initial assumptions were incorrect because we were working with limited knowledge. No one knew how shipwrights designed and constructed this type of ship. On the first day I could see it was an eighteenth-century merchant ship, one that was larger than average for colonial America. As we excavated and uncovered hundreds of details major and minor, a complete three-dimensional image of the ship slowly developed in our minds. Only upon completion of the fieldwork did we have the information and the luxury of time to develop a descriptive overview of the vessel, analyze the data gathered, and determine how the shipwright designed and built the vessel.

A GENERAL DESCRIPTION OF THE SHIP

When sailed in the eighteenth century this ship was a three-masted merchantman, approximately one hundred feet long overall, eighty-two feet long on the main deck, with a maximum breadth of twenty-four feet. It would have been registered at 130–200 tons, depending on the formula used at the city of registry. This was a large merchant ship for colonial America but within the range of cargo vessels plying the Atlantic Ocean.

The main cargo hold was a large open area forty-four feet long, twenty-two feet wide, and nine feet deep. Close to the mainmast, which was stepped at the deepest part of the hold, were two bilge pumps, surrounded by a large wooden planked box. Other than those, the main cargo hold was free of any structures.

A colonial merchant ship similar to, but larger than the Ronson ship. Detail from A view of New York from Brooklyn Heights (William Burgis, c. 1717). *Collection of the New-York Historical Society, image 32098.*

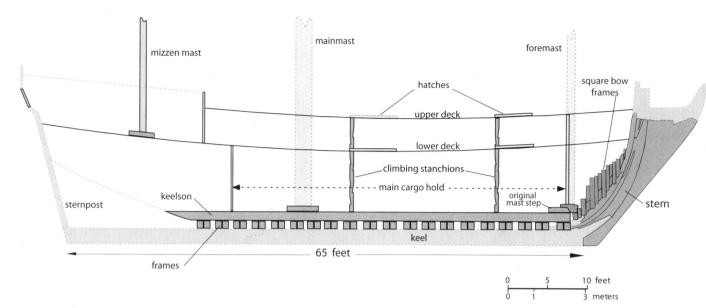

Side cutaway of the ship's layout. Light gray timbers were derived from the evidence, but had not survived or were inaccessible at the site. *Illustration by Warren Riess.*

We found no indications of stanchions to support the deck beams above, except one at each corner of the cargo hatches. Forward and aft of the main hold were smaller storage areas. The forward compartment appeared to have been used for general ships stowage, for there we found a tar tub and brush, a pulley block, and a few other ship hardware artifacts. The aft compartment was lined with tongue-and-grooved pine planking, a detail to protect moisture-sensitive stores such as flour and gunpowder. There, embedded in the pine planking, we discovered a lead pistol ball, whether fired in anger or accidentally we could not tell.

Remnants of mast steps indicate that the ship was "ship-rigged"; that is, having three masts, with square sails on the main and foremasts and a fore-and-aft lateen sail on the mizzen mast. The hull had a bluff bow compared to more modern ships and was quite flat on the bottom. It reached maximum breadth about thirty feet aft of the bow, remained at full breadth for twenty-four feet, and then slowly tapered toward the stern. The ship was built for maximum cargo capacity rather than speed.

The ship's relatively flat bottom provided several advantages and held disadvantages as well. For the same amount of cargo space, the ship drew less water than a V- or rounded-hulled ship. Its shallow draft allowed it to sail into most bays, rivers, and harbors. Under normal trade wind sailing, with a good wind off its quarter, a flat-bottomed ship tended to sail fairly level

and was slower to get into trouble if a sudden squall struck. This was an asset that allowed the ship to sail with a slightly smaller crew, thereby saving costs for the owner. However, flat-bottomed ships typically did not sail as well as others when the wind was not behind them or in the midst of a storm. Without a deep keel they tended to crab, or skid a bit sideways with the wind, and were usually not able to sail as close into the wind as other ships.

One main, or lower, deck ran the length of the ship, just above the normal waterline. Below it were the cargo hold and the fore and aft stowage areas. Above it were a central area often called *'tween decks*, for more cargo and four small cannon, a forecastle (*fo'c's'le*) for the crew, and an after cabin for the officers. We found two gunports and a smaller loading port through the hull on the port side. Excavating the starboard side was not possible, but we assume it was similar. Above this central area was the weather, or upper, deck that would be the *waist* of the ship. On the centerline of the ship, one in front of the other, were two cargo hatches on each of the upper and lower decks.

A few upper deck beams and their supporting knees were still in place above the main cargo hold. They indicate an approximate 4½ feet between the lower and upper decks amidships. However, we found no indication of the height of the upper deck in the bow and stern. It appeared that they were cut down when the eighteenth-century developers filled the site. On most British eighteenth-century ships the upper deck stepped up in the bow and stern to provide more head-room in the stern cabin and forecastle, whereas on some the upper deck was one continuous sweep the entire length of the ship.

When building a ship, the first major timber that the shipwright laid down was the keel, the ship's back-bone. Unfortunately, during the excavation we were only able to touch blindly the top of the keel beneath the cargo hold. From the position of other timbers one can determine that it was approximately sixty-five feet long. It is doubtful that a span this long would have been cut from one timber, but how many pieces were joined together to make up the keel length we will never know. At that time British and British colonial keels were usually made of oak or elm.

The keel was one of the few straight heavy timbers on a wooden ship. Most of the ship's timbers were at least slightly curved, as were the deck beams, while others formed much tighter arcs and even semi-S curves. For strength a shipwright needed to choose a timber in which the grain followed a curve, rather than cutting across a grain to create a shape. Heat-ing and forcing wood to a new form works for planks but not for thicker timbers because, the wood at the outside of the curve will typically rip apart. Therefore, a shipwright would create a list of curved *compass timbers* he would require for a particular ship, survey a forest to buy trees that possessed the arced oak limbs and roots to satisfy his list, and finally trim structural

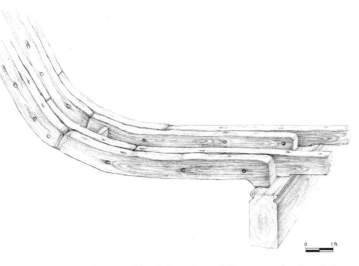

Typical frames of the ship in the midships area, showing their fore-and-aft fastenings. *Illustration by Kathleen Galligan.*

timbers from the naturally curved sections of the trees.

After laying down the keel, to continue the heavy timber up into the bow, the shipwrights attached a stem to the forward end of the keel. For this ship the complete stem was made of two naturally curved oak timbers. The lower stem piece measured 14 feet, 2 inches long, with a varying cross section of 14 to 16 inches. The lower stem timber was attached to the keel with an overlapping joint known as a flat scarf. A rab-bet was carved into each side of the stem to accept the forward ends of the ship's outer planking. Inside of the stem, running parallel and bolted to it was an apron. Forward of the stem, on the outside of the hull, was the knee of the head, the first of many timbers that consti-tuted the ship's *beak* or *prow*.

At the aft end of the keel, it was common for West-ern shipwrights to attach a sternpost that was the cen-ter timber for the stern. They did so with a mortise and tenon and supported the almost ninety-degree joint with a large stern knee. Because most of the vessel's stern lay on the street side of the boundary, we were not able to excavate down to the sternpost. However, we did tunnel horizontally to it and observed its top when the ship was torn apart. In cross section it was a hefty 12½ by 11 inches, with a rabbet on either side surface to accept the aft ends of the outer planking.

Lying on top of and perpendicular to the keel were thirty-five heavy oak frames. Each frame of the ship was composed of a floor timber and several futtocks. The futtocks and floor timbers varied in size but had an average square cross section of 8½ by 8½ inches. The space between the frames averaged only 6 inches. These dimensions varied for each frame, especially in the bow and stern. In the bow the frames were thicker and left little or no space between them.

The bow's construction was complex—one of the most interesting human achievements I have seen in forty-four years of archaeology. Unlike later ships' bows that were made with frames canting forward, there were no cant frames in the bow. There were only square frames bolted more than halfway up the stem, with the remaining forward space filled with hawse pieces. The bow frames therefore needed severe bevel-ing on their outside and inside surfaces to provide a proper surface for planking. Their fore and aft faces were also beveled and shaped to match the next frame so that they fitted together obliquely. These were ex-traordinary pieces, chosen to match the curves of the bow while having four surfaces on which cut bevels independently changed to match the shipwright's construction needs.

Between frames in the central part of the ship, just above the turn of the bilge, we found 2-inch thick boards, or chocks, their outer edges resting on the outer planking but their inner edges 1 inch short of the ceiling planks (inner hull planks). We do not know whether they acted only as spacers during construction, kept water and sand in the bilge from quickly shifting when the ship rolled in heavy weather, prevented salt packed between the frames for hull preservation from shifting into the bilge, or had some other function or a combination of these.

On top of the frames, parallel to the keel, lay the impressive oak keelson. It was 12 inches wide, 14 inches high, and 56 feet long. We were not able to inspect all of it because of the two remaining athwartship safety walls, so we do not know if it was made of one or more timbers. The shipwrights secured the keelson, frames, keel, and stem together with sturdy iron drift pins.

Outer planks for the ship were sawn out of oak, were generally 2 inches thick, and varied in width from 8 to 14 inches. Except for a very few places, we found them still tightly joined to frames and caulked. They were mostly fastened to each frame with two octagonal oak trunnels (wooden dowels), which were diagonally offset and continued inside to fasten the ceiling planks also. Trunnels were used in wooden shipbuilding and elsewhere, such as buildings and furniture, in place of metal to form a tight, noncorroding fastener.

An interesting detail, for which we have found no explanation, was the existence of iron concretions on the inside of the strake of planking next to the keel (*garboard strake*). Approximately halfway between frames in the midships cargo hold, Sheli recorded what might have been the head of a spike or bolt, indicating that an iron fastener had existed through the garboard strake between frames to attach something on its outside surface. Though a number of possibilities come to mind, we have yet to discover in the archival or archaeological records another seventeenth- or eighteenth-century ship with such a feature.

Farther away from the keel, just above the waterline and below the gunports, three strakes of wales (double-thick outer planking) were in a solid belt, which girdled the vessel from the stem to the stern tuck. Opposite the wales, inside the hull, was a matching belt of double-thick ceiling planks called *clamps*. This belt of

thick wood helped stiffen the ship longitudinally and strengthened it where the deck beams rested. Another single wale and clamp belt existed approximately four feet above it to support the upper deck beams.

A layer of pitch and hair, approximately half an inch thick, coated the outside surface of the outer planking below the waterline. Fastened with iron nails over that layer, still surviving in some places, was a sheathing of one-inch softwood planks, called *firring* or *sheathing*. These two outer layers further waterproofed the hull and effectively held at bay shipworms and other woodborers from the more permanent oak planks. Woodborers could attack the firring boards but ideally would not be able to get through to the main hull. Crew or shipyard workers stripped off the sheathing and pitch every few years as needed and replaced them with new material.

Only approximately half of the sheathing remained on the ship's port side, outside the outer planking, and what remained was well rotted. The remaining sheathing on the hull was honeycombed with shipworm holes, yet few structural timbers showed damage from the woodborers. Since much of the sheathing was missing, though that side was covered by fill soon after it was spiked in place, it would imply that the sheathing was rotting off the ship, and not being replaced, while the vessel was floating in the harbor for at least a few years. Sutherland's 1717 statement that sheathing might be serviceable in oceanic sailing for up to seven years, discussions with Manhattan archaeologists who studied the island's eighteenth-century planked cribbing, and the inspection of more modern wooden derelicts strongly support the possibility that the ship was kept in the harbor for one or two decades before being buried.

The inside surface of the hull frames was completely covered with ceiling planking, clamps, and limber boards. In addition, the ship had three breast hooks, which were internal structural timbers to tie both sides of the ship together at the bow. The lowest breast hook was the smallest, made from a single large curved timber. The second breast hook, or deck shelf, was made of three timbers and bolted just under the main deck. A shelf was cut into its upper surface to support the deck. Another large breast hook, hewn from a single timber, was bolted above the deck. A fourth timber, probably a deck shelf, was approximately four feet above the other shelf.

Although there were three masts on the Ronson ship, we located only the foremast and mainmast partners (heavy support timbers in the deck) because of the original demolition of the deck in the stern. There were three openings in the mainmast partners. The largest was for the mainmast, while two smaller holes would have held two bilge pumps, stepped behind the mast on either side. We recovered the octagonal butt of the mizzen mast and the butt of the port bilge pump—a simple hand-powered device common on eighteenth-century ships. Its tube was made by boring a hole down the center of a yellow pine log.[1]

Each of the ship's three masts was stepped differently. The foremast step was a heavy semi-rectangular timber that fitted over and was attached to the keelson. Most of it was in the foundation wall just behind the bow, but we could see that it was splayed open, with the starboard side slightly lifted. Probably because of that damage, a second foremast step had been added just forward, and overlapping on top of the first. Though it also was shaped to fit the other timbers, it was fastened with an odd mixture of iron fasteners. The mainmast step was a rectilinear hole in the keelson, reinforced with timbers to either side. The mizzen mast step was aft of that, resting in the centerline on the lower deck, mostly within the safety wall just aft of the main cargo hold.

Below the lower deck we found remnants of bulkheads (internal walls) that separated the central cargo hold from other compartments. The forwardmost bulkhead was ten feet aft of the bow and there were indications of another bulkhead eight feet aft of the mainmast. The partitioning separated the interior of the hull into at least three large compartments: a bow storage space, which may have been partitioned further, a main hold for the cargo, and an aft storage space that was compartmentalized for provisions and munitions. We found no evidence of temporary bulkheads in the forty-four-foot-long central cargo hold. Above the hold, between decks in the amidships area, nail holes on the lower deck suggest temporary partitioning of that space for cargo and stores.

The care with which the shipwright had built the ship was impressive. We saw no indications of any labor-saving shortcuts taken. We did notice that the builder had not always used a perfect piece of timber for a structural member, and the spacing of frames was not as systematic as we expected from having studied eighteenth-century naval ship remains and building plans. Yet there was evidence that the ship had made, and obviously survived, transoceanic voyages.

It seemed as if the shipwright was resourceful in using what curved timbers he could obtain and shifting their position a bit when necessary to build a properly shaped, strong ship.

STUDYING THE SHIP

The ship remains posed many questions that would set in motion a series of investigative analyses. When we left Manhattan some of us spent months organizing the artifacts, ship timbers, and data. Joan Geismar's New York team continued with the artifact analyses, Betty Seifert's Massachusetts team initiated the conservation processes, and I commenced a long-term study of the ship.

Historians have not known much about these ships, and I wanted to see if this ship's remains could answer some questions about the ship's design, construction, ownership, origins, usage, and final resting place. I was aware that in the eighteenth century a prospective owner's contract with the shipwright was usually simple. It recorded that the ship would be a particular size and shape, and then a price and payment were detailed. Then the shipwright might or might not draw the ship plan prior to starting construction. Depending upon availability of timbers, the ship he built might not exactly match his design. Yet the ship remains we were studying, after years of use on the ocean and more than two centuries buried below Manhattan, were not going to have the same shape as they did when the ship was built. Having only the timbers, I needed to piece this puzzle together working chronologically backward, from the evidence we uncovered, to the ship as it sailed, as it was built, as it was designed by the shipwright, and finally as it was conceived by the would be owner(s).

In June 1982 we gathered an interdisciplinary team of specialists from around the United States to help extract information from the artifacts and field data. Sheli, in charge of recording the site, conducted a preliminary study of the hull. She was hindered, and we were frustrated many times during the site analysis, because just as we left Manhattan, someone in the New York laboratory inadvertently discarded two boxes of her belongings, including her field notebook. The notebook contained many diagnostic field sketches and notes, including correlations of all of the field site data recorded by separate teams. If we had copied our field notes each evening we would have been fine. If we had replaced the site illustrator when he left, the site plan would have included most of the information graphically. But ifs do not count. We spent approximately four months working backward through other data to reconstruct sufficient information from the lost notebook to develop a general plan of the site for a field report. Appending hundreds of details would necessitate much more of my time in the future.

In the interim, within the relative luxury of the conservation laboratory, it was possible to examine the saved bow timbers closely for the first time. Armed with field notes, the laboratory team confirmed all of the identification tags, carefully cleaned each timber, and launched a thorough documentation. A meticulous recording of the timbers was necessary for several reasons. While we intended to use the best conservation methods available, there were no guarantees that every timber would retain its shape when dried. Thorough records, drawings, full-scale tracings, and photographs would ensure reconstruction, should we lose any timbers in the conservation processes. Furthermore, scrupulous details were important for accurate research modeling. To reconstruct the bow in a museum we intended first to carve a scale model of each piece and construct a working model of the bow, discovering new information and mistakes in recording and analysis in the process.

To produce the full-scale traces, Kerry Horn employed a method developed by J. Richard Steffy at the Institute of Nautical Archaeology. She suspended a large piece of glass over a timber, spread a clear sheet of plastic over the glass, and carefully traced the outline of the timber with indelible felt-tipped pens. She color-coded and traced details such as nail holes, trunnel holes, and wood grain.

Jay Rosloff, then a graduate student in nautical archaeology at Texas A&M University, studied the ship's bow as his master's thesis project. Using 1:10 copies of Kerry's traces, he carved a scale model of each timber and plank of the bow, then constructed a model of the bow, cleverly determining how it might be reconstructed in a museum, and conducted historical research in an attempt to identify the ship's nationality by the shape of the bow. Although unsuccessful in the identification attempt with information from the bow only, Jay found that this section provided important new details about how an eighteenth-century shipwright might build a successful ship while not following the published rules.[2]

Also at Texas A&M, S. Ruby Lang cataloged the wood recording team's hundreds of photographs, drawings, and references to allow us to locate and inspect the records of each recorded piece easily. In the field, Ruby had co-directed the wood recording team with Jay Rosloff. Chronicling their knowledge and using it to catalog diagnostic data was an essential step toward preservation and analysis.

The woods used in the ship timbers and their condition needed to be established for various reasons. Betty Seifert's conservation processes were dependent upon the species and chemical and water content of the material to be preserved, and my historical analysis would depend to some extent on the species of woods used to build the ship. In addition, the eventual reconstruction of the ship's bow would require knowledge of the relative physical strength and stability of the treated wood. For these reasons and more, we sent small samples of some timbers and trunnels to the University of Maine's Forestry Department, where Dr. Richard Jagels identified the wood and conducted chemical and physical strength analyses experiments on the samples.

Jagels found that the ship's wood had deteriorated so much that it was weaker and more plastic than one might expect from its weight. The oak structural members had lost approximately 75 percent of their

Kerry Horn made 1:1 tracings of each surface of the saved timbers. She recorded details using a color code to identify such things as nail and trunnel holes, tool marks, and shipworm damage. *Photo by Betty Seifert, courtesy of the Mariners' Museum.*

strength. Each timber could hold its own weight, but if the bow were reconstructed we would have to add supports so that the lower pieces would not have to support the rest of the timbers. More plasticity meant the pieces would bend under a load but not return to their original position if the load were removed. They would be permanently deformed if bent. This knowledge was important not only for the final bow reconstruction but also for planning how we were to move and store the pieces throughout the conservation process.

In the summer of 1982 Sheli and I finished our field report, which contained an overview of the site and the research to date, then returned to graduate school at the Universities of Pennsylvania and New Hampshire respectively. Between scholastic requirements Sheli returned to the projects in which she had already been involved, while I carried on with the analysis and research of the Manhattan ship for my doctoral thesis. The more I studied it, the more intrigued I became.

THOUGHTS ON THE SHAPE OF THE SHIP

Necessity being the mother of invention, and humans being a resourceful lot by nature, when a specific need in water transportation arose, people throughout history created a type of vessel designed to fit that need. I felt that the development of uniquely designed ships to transport cargoes particular to the American colonies across the Atlantic, as shown in the Ronson ship's remains, might illuminate at least one area of ship design development. For example, if we were to consider John Sand's early suggestion that it might be an American tobacco ship, we must look at the tobacco trade, which was unlike any other. Because of the high value of the cargo, strict laws were established to ensure the quality of the tobacco when it reached market in England and Scotland. In the early eighteenth century, the sizes of tobacco hogsheads (large casks) were legally standardized in each colony, and tobacco inspection was instituted. Ships' cargo holds were made watertight, and the ships usually traveled in convoy, escorted by a British warship. In order to cut transportation costs before 1730, tobacco ships sometimes picked up their cargo at a plantation site along the upper river banks, instead of at such Chesapeake entrepôts as Williamsburg or Yorktown.[3]

In the seventeenth century, before tobacco was tightly compressed into hogsheads, a cargo of tobacco was light for its volume. Captured Dutch flyboats

(flouts or flutes), which were noted for their high stowage volume per tons burden (capacity), were often used in the tobacco trade. Flyboats were efficient but not good tobacco ships as they were not well armed, especially for the transatlantic trade. True, the tobacco ships generally crossed the Atlantic under convoy of a royal warship, but these were not always all the protection they needed, and the warships were not always available. In the eighteenth century, when packers began to compress tobacco into the hogsheads to ship more tobacco leaves per volume, one of the most important advantages of the flyboats was eliminated. Virginia port records show that few flyboats were used in the eighteenth century. Whether the early eighteenth-century tobacco ships were the same as the common English merchant frigates or colliers, or were similar to the continental flyboats, is not evident in existing documents. We know little about any of the early eighteenth-century merchantmen. Because of this, it was important to analyze the New York ship comparatively to try to determine whether it was designed and built to be a tobacco vessel.[4]

Comparing the hull configurations of the various known ship types to the general shape of our hull, the Ronson ship appeared to be a combination of an English merchant frigate and a Dutch flyboat. Ships' hulls can be longitudinally divided into three basic sections: the bow, midship, and stern. Although all three parts of the hull perform a number of duties, each has a specific effect on the ship's motion through the water.

A ship's bow must move the water that is in front of the hull in order for the ship to proceed. A blunt bow provides more cargo space and buoyancy but pushes the water in front of it, forming a bow wave, and the water in the bow wave flows to either side. Constantly pushing the water up into the bow wave draws much energy from the ship's power and therefore slows the ship. A sharp bow pushes the water to either side of the ship, using less energy than the blunt bow because it moves the water more horizontally than vertically. Although the sharp bow is more efficient in terms of speed and power, other functions—such as cargo capacity, necessary buoyancy to keep the bow from diving in rough seas, and shape of the rest of the ship— often determined which type of bow was needed in the eighteenth century.

The midship section of a hull was generally determined by necessary cargo capacity and draft (depth in the water). Flat floors (full bottoms) provided for

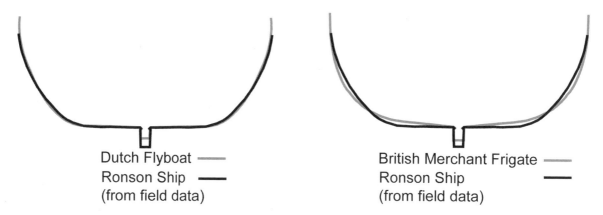

Dutch Flyboat ——
Ronson Ship ——
(from field data)

British Merchant Frigate ——
Ronson Ship ——
(from field data)

Central cargo area of the Ronson ship compared to a typical flyboat and a typical merchant frigate. Flyboat and frigate lines from Fredrik Henrik af Chapman, Architectura Navalis Mercatoria (Stockholm, 1768; repr. New York: Praeger, 1968), plates LII and LIII. Illustration by Warren Riess.

maximum volume for cargo per depth of hold and more stability when a loaded ship was left aground by tides in a shallow area. However, flat floors did not provide a deep keel to help the ship sail closer to the wind. A *V-shaped* hull provided better sailing and speed characteristics for the ship but at the expense of cargo capacity per draft.

A hull's stern has a similar but opposite purpose to the bow. It closes the hole in the water created by the bow after the midship section has passed through it. If the stern is full, it causes a partial vacuum as the ship moves forward, slowing the ship. But a full stern in a merchant vessel provides cargo capacity. A sharp stern allows the water to come together easily behind the ship, but it allows for little cargo space.

Flyboats and merchant frigates possessed significantly different hull shapes. A flyboat's bow was fully round above and below the water line when viewed from above. From the side, the flyboat bow's profile entered the water almost vertically, then curved back to meet the flat floors of the midship section. The midship cross section was almost square, with relatively flat floors and almost vertical sides. The stern continued the full shape of the bow and midship area, providing an almost rectangular outline of the ship when seen from above. Its bow pushed the water in front of the hull as the ship moved forward and the stern did not allow for an easy closure of the water behind the hull. The flyboat's shape offered maximum cargo capacity for a given length, breadth, and depth of hull. Its flat floors provided more stability in the face of a sudden squall, allowing flyboats to be manned by

a smaller crew—a cost-saving benefit augmented by a simpler sail configuration. However, its shape and sail configuration rendered it most useful for slower transport in friendly waters.

When compared to a flyboat, a frigate's underwater bow was relatively sharp when seen from below and relatively vertical when seen in profile. As the entrance mechanism for the V-shaped midship section, the sharp bow pushed the water to either side. Since the bow was not required to meet flat floors in the midship section, the lower end of the bow was not required to curve back like that of the flyboat. Speed and agility were more important than great cargo capacity, therefore both the upper and lower bow areas were fairly sharp (though not as sharp as in nineteenth- and twentieth-century ships). The frigate's deeper bow added a little cargo capacity and buoyancy to the bow, but not enough to give the bow the same buoyancy or stowage capacity as those of the flyboat. However, the more vertical bow did effectively provide a longer keel forward, which gave the frigate more speed and the ability to sail closer to the wind. The frigate's midship section offered speed and sailing ability in exchange for a lower cargo capacity, but the capacity was not drastically low. The frigate's stern was often *square tucked,* which was much sharper underwater than the round-sterned flyboats. In total, the merchant frigates provided a relatively fast and agile ship to carry a reasonable amount of cargo, while the flyboats provided more stowage volume at the cost of speed and maneuverability.

The shape of the Ronson ship was not typical of

what we know of either the flyboats or frigates. It seems to have been a combination of the two. The midship area was similar to that of the flyboats, with their relatively flat floors, hard turn at the bilge, and relatively flat curve above the floors. The Ronson ship's cargo stowage volume was therefore large in relation to her draft or in relation to the stowage volume of a merchant frigate of similar length and beam.

The Ronson ship's bow appears to be a compromise between that of a merchant frigate and that of a flyboat. Viewed from above, the ship's underwater bow was not as full as that of a flyboat. It was rounded but did not reach maximum breadth quickly. However, the ship's bow had to meet its midsection, which had flat floors. In order to accomplish this, the bow profile, except for the bottom few feet, looked much like that of a flyboat, curving in depth to meet the depth of the midship's flat floors. The stem profile was drawn to be a true arc of 16-foot radius at the rabbet where the hull planking terminated. This precluded providing the hull form with the fine entrance needed to sail close to the wind. Some reverse curve was obtained in the lower sections of the forward frames to provide a certain degree of fineness, but the bluntness of the bow did not allow for a fast ship. The fullness provided maximum cargo capacity, which was the purpose of the vessel, but which also limited maneuverability. The extension of deadwood below the waterline and forward of the curved stem piece made some improvement in the sailing qualities.

The stern of the Ronson ship was a familiar square tucked stern of an English merchant frigate. Its upper structure was wide, while below water its deadwood section quickly narrowed to the width of the keel. The square tucked stern offered very little stowage space, but provided a long keel structure for speed and sailing ability.

The Ronson ship's design therefore appears to be an adaptation of an early eighteenth-century British merchant frigate, as influenced by the Dutch and French flyboats. Its design may answer Ralph Davis's question, raised in *The Rise of the English Shipping Industry in The 17th and 18th Century*, about how British ships became more efficient in the eighteenth century. Davis surmised that British merchant ship builders studied Dutch and French flyboats that were captured in the War of Spanish Succession (1702–13), to develop more efficient transatlantic cargo vessels, but he could not determine how it was accomplished.[5]

The development or trial of this type of ship in the early eighteenth century appears logical in retrospect. British merchants and shipwrights alike knew the qualities and drawbacks of their frigates as well as those of the flyboats. If the combination worked well, the ship would retain much of the frigate's speed, agility, and defensive fighting ability, while being able to carry more cargo into shallow areas. This design combination might be excellent for the southern colonial and Netherlands trades, where limited protection, cargo capacity, and shallow draft were all useful. Every ship was a balance of factors that often were opposed to each other. The Ronson ship's overall shape and dimensions revealed which qualities the architect and owner felt were most important for the ship. Several seventeenth- and eighteenth-century authors addressed the problem, but Fredrik af Chapman was the most succinct:

A MERCHANT SHIP OUGHT:

1. To be able to carry a great lading in proportion to its size.
2. To sail well by the wind, in order to beat easily off a coast where it may be embayed, and also to come about well in a hollow sea [a sea with steep waves].
3. To work with a crew small in number in proportion to its cargo.
4. To be able to sail with a small quantity of ballast.[6]

The Ronson ship appears to have been a compromise of Chapman's qualities. The ship probably held a large amount of cargo per length and crew size, sailed reasonably well to beat off a lee shore, carried a press of sail in a strong wind, and carried less ballast than some other ships of her size. These properties were accomplished with the ship's great breadth-to-length ratio (1:3.4), full bottom, full upper bow, and long keel (compared to other full-bodied cargo ships). The longer keel offset some of the poor sailing properties of the flat bottom. Though the Ronson ship's master may have wanted to sail with more than a minimum crew, to enable them to fight off small privateers and pirates, the ship's full bottom provided enough space to allow a good cargo tonnage-per-man ratio for economy. In addition, the flat bottom required less ballast because the shape of the hull lessened its tendency to heel. In theory, the Ronson ship was an exceptionally good compromise.

I have found no information in archival or

archaeological sources to indicate if the Ronson ship type of hull continued to be built. If the ship had been built from memory, with just a few preshaped "mold frames," one might infer that it was a traditional hull. However, fore-and-aft trunnels in every one of this ship's frames are clues that the hull was not built that way. We can tell that the shape of each frame was designed and built before being erected in place, because otherwise the shipwrights would not have been able to drive the fore-and-aft trunnels into their holes. Therefore the ship could have had a standard, experimental, or prototype hull.

Some documentary evidence does imply that more ships were constructed to a similar design. A Captain Stevens in 1748 stated, "In time of war, ships are built sharp, and in time of peace, full [referring to the shape of the midship cross section] . . . most ships are now built in such a manner as to take the ground loaded"; that is, flat bottomed.[7]

Captain Stevens's statement may be a clue to the historical milieu at the time of the Ronson ship's creation. Although not as full as the flyboats, which plied safer waters than the Western Atlantic, the Ronson ship was fairly full. Stevens's statement therefore implies that the ship may have been built in time of peace. Since we could see evidence at the site that the ship had been used for several years and we knew from the historical records and maps that it was buried circa 1750, I surmised that the vessel was possibly built after the War of Spanish Succession, which ended in 1713, and before the War of Jenkins' Ear, which began in 1739.

The ship's remains also offered information about the development of the bow framing in wooden ships. As noted, ships' bows varied in shape from sharp to bluff. The Ronson ship's bow, which was moderately bluff, required frames to form a solid, almost complete surface, shaped to allow side planking to turn inward to end at the stem. The proper shape could be accomplished using either cant or square frames, but the builder chose to use square frames.

Cant frames simplified the transition from the hull's fore-and-aft sides to the stem by being at an angle to the keel. The frames' angles changed systematically from perpendicular to the keel toward parallel to the keel as they were placed nearer the stem. From above, they looked a bit like an opened fan. Since cant frames absorb the shock of storm waves on the bow better than square frames, fewer frames were needed

when using cant frames and thus bow construction could be lighter while retaining the same strength. The builder also would use timbers with less cross section than those for square frames, saving money and available timber.[8]

Square frames were perpendicular to the keel, like the midship frames. To accomplish the proper form near the stem, bow square frames had to be placed up the stem apron and the final space near the stem filled with hawse pieces. The inner surfaces of square frames needed to be drastically beveled to provide a surface for the planks. Because bow square frames provided little support by themselves against wave shock on the bow, the frames and the hawse pieces in this ship were reinforced with chocks and massive breast hooks to form a bow of almost solid timber.

The use of square frames in the ship is important when attempting to document the development of hull construction. Although cant frames have been used on ships since the third century BC, there was a period of some seven centuries when square frames were used. Sometime around the eleventh century AD, as large ships developed, shipwrights began to use square frames in the bow.[9] Yet by the mid-eighteenth century square frames were not used, and only cant frames appear in literature and ship remains. In 1935 Howard Chapelle, studying the development of American ships, placed the reintroduction of the exclusive use of cant frames to between 1650 and 1750.[10] The Ronson ship, built in the first half of the eighteenth century, represents the latest indication for the continued use of square frames. Thus the ship was evidence that the dates for the elimination of square frames probably were further narrowed to somewhere between 1700 and 1739. Subsequent research was to narrow that time spread.

DETERMINING THE HULL'S SHAPE

Except for some general information about shapes, the method used to design early eighteenth-century merchant ships has not been known. Shipwrights jealously guarded their secrets until metal shipbuilding in the nineteenth century. In fact, each of the eighteenth-century naval architects and shipwrights may have used a different method. Was it possible to replicate the shipwright's original plan of the Manhattan ship? In order to attempt it I would have to work backward from the ship's remains to the original design. I needed, first, to make a detailed three-dimensional plan of the ship as we found it, somewhat out of shape after years of sailing and centuries of compression in Manhattan; second, to determine the hull's shape as built; third, to determine the ship designer's method; and fourth, to derive the shipwright's original plan. One might assume that the shipwright's design and constructed ship would be identical. However, working with large timbers that could not be bent far without severely weakening them, the shipwright needed to use naturally curved timbers, and he might not have found exactly what he wanted to match the design. One can see from the remains we studied that differences in curvature and unfortunate knot locations forced this shipwright to shift frames and other heavy timbers to produce a slightly different but still strong hull.

An early general drawing and description was not difficult in the summer of 1982, but determining an accurately constructed shape of the hull, called the *ship's lines*, turned into a frustrating, lengthy endeavor. On the site I drove an eight-inch spike into the asphalt to establish our primary datum, or benchmark, from which all things are measured. I then established a baseline from that, roughly parallel to the ship's keel. As the baseline was compromised a few times by the nearby construction crew, each excavation team established secondary datum points near their section to give them something local from which to take their measurements. When we excavated deeper into the ship each team needed to establish new, lower datum points. I had each excavation team's field notebook and drawings, with all the distances from the baseline, measurement grids, and secondary datum points, but the exact locations of the datum, secondary datum points, and baseline on any day were lost when, as mentioned, a cleaning crew inadvertently threw out a key notebook at the end of the fieldwork.

I spent hundreds of hours systematically working backward, using geometry, graphics, scaled photographs projected on the wall, and field illustrations to determine each datum's location and then reconstructed on paper each section of the ship for each day. Nothing fitted well. It was as if the datum points were floating around, more horizontally than vertically, within an eight-inch space. Their positions determined backward from measurements taken in the morning did not match those taken that afternoon or the next

morning. There was no sense in forcing the data to fit; a serious mistake existed somewhere that I could not find. I checked and rechecked my work, asked others to look for mistakes, became frustrated time and again, and sometimes abandoned the entire project for a year or more before returning to the conundrum. Years went by as I addressed my duties as a research professor at the University of Maine, working on various archaeology and history projects and teaching undergraduate and graduate students.

After approximately fifteen years, representing six serious attempts at solving the puzzle, I determined to take a summer of immersion in the project to construct a working (rough) scale model of each piece of recorded wood to see if fitting them together would help solve the mystery. After all, the ship was a bit misshapen by more than two centuries of burial, so the pieces might join together to reveal the shape more clearly than the troublesome field data. Doing so had worked for Jay Rosloff's bow analysis, though he had much more detailed data from the 1:1 tracings of the bow timbers. I had decent but necessarily leaner data on the rest of the ship's timbers taken outside in the mud during the fieldwork.

At the start of the summer as I prepared to start the model I had the good fortune of receiving a grant to hire as an intern for two summers Carrie Atkins, an intelligent and focused undergraduate student at Bowdoin College. She quickly assimilated how to translate the field data into wooden scale models of each timber and plank. Using the pieces, along with my drawings and Bob Adams's field photographs, she constructed a 1:30 model of the ship as built, proving and disproving various conclusions I had drawn and finding new solutions when my deductions did not work. Yet two major questions remained. First, the forward end of the midship area did not perfectly match the aft end of the bow model she made based on Jay's analysis. Second, while Carrie had fitted together the model timber pieces convincingly, the question still remained: why did the data show the datum points floating around? Until those two puzzles were solved I could not assume we had an accurate shape of the ship as constructed.

The solution to both questions came one evening during a conversation with Jay about the discrepancy between his and Carrie's models. He reminded me that Sheli's team had taken the data for the aft frames of the bow just minutes before we noticed that the mud walls in the bow were slumping in. He pointed out that there was every chance the last frame they measured had shifted in, not enough to be noticed in the field, but enough to cause a difference in the two models. Upon inspecting all the bow field notes I could see that this was precisely what had happened, including Sheli's team having to set up their measuring device differently in that spot.

I started to wonder if the bow situation was connected to the wandering data points problem, and two weeks later the puzzle pieces in my mind seemed to snap together all at once. During the fieldwork every night we had needed to let the groundwater refill the ship's hull to keep the wood and fill from freezing, and every morning we pumped the water out to work. As we excavated deeper into the ship the hydrostatic pressure, caused by the groundwater pressing in on the hull, increased during the day and was equalized at night by the water seeping in. The ship, made of centuries-old saturated oak, was perhaps changing shape during the course of each day and night, but so slowly that we never noticed it in the field.

With this possibility in mind I went back to the data for the main cargo hold, where one might expect a greater change because there was a longer expanse of hull without support. Assuming now that the primary datum points outside the ship were stationary and all the field data were correct, the excavation teams' recordings showed a hull that seemed to be slowly breathing, taking one long irregular breath each day, while we worked inside oblivious to the slow motion. The most obvious difference was that during each day in the last two weeks of excavation, the side of the hull stretched inward more at the middle than at the top or bottom. To us it appeared as if the side of the hull was designed at each station with two sweeps of different radii, while in fact it had been constructed as one large arc. Many years of frustration then slowly dissolved, finally allowing me confidently to finish drawing the ship as it had been constructed and used in the eighteenth century.

HOW WAS THE SHIP DESIGNED?

Several seventeenth- and eighteenth-century authors wrote about designing and building ships in northern Europe, but only five shipwrights published some level of detail of their design techniques. They were Edmund Bushnell (1669), Anthony Deane

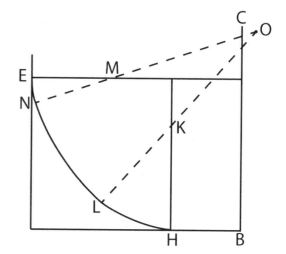

Deane's method of designing the midships cross section of a warship, using time-tested proportions. His ship's centerline is line CB. The curve from E to H is three arcs with different radii. The arc from N to L had a radius of 20/36 of the maximum breadth of the ship, with a center at O. *Illustration by Warren Riess.*

(1670), William Sutherland (1711), Mungo Murray (1754), and Fredrik af Chapman (1768).[11]

Bushnell and Deane each described in a few pages their own geometric method of designing a warship in 1670. They started by choosing a length and maximum breadth and then with straight lines and various arcs, which are sections of circles, they drew an outline of the ship from the side (sheer plan), an outline from the top (half-breadth), and then a series of cross sections (stations) overlapping to describe the hull shape every few feet. Bushnell and Deane, describing their own method of drafting a warship, at first described how to find the necessary dimensions graphically, then using simple mathematics. Each shipwright offered the lengths of the straight lines, radii of each arc, and various angles that they had determined through experience, as sometimes complex fractions of the length of the keel or maximum breadth of the hull (B). For example, Deane determined the radius of one arc to be 20/36 B and the rake of the sternpost to be 11/72 B.

The fact that the shipwright's men built the Ronson ship's frames before they erected them, indicated by fore-and-aft trunnels, implied that each frame was part of a drawn design that the shipwright used for construction. But did the ship's designer use a geometric technique similar to Bushnell's or Deane's? Their methods created a ship's cross section and side view that were combinations of simple arcs and straight lines. Determining straight lines on a drawing of part of the Manhattan ship was simple. However the method of determining if a curve was part of a circle, and finding its center and radius, at first puzzled me. Maclean Shakshober, a retired naval architect, showed me a simple method he had developed to study the hull cross sections of HMS *Mary Rose*. Using his technique I drew a series of lines inside and perpendicular to the outline of the hull at several frame stations. The lines represented possible radii of arcs. I discovered that the lines crossed at two or three distinct points inboard of the ship at each station. These points corresponded in principle to those described by Bushnell and Deane, but they were in different positions than for the two shipwrights' warship plans. It appeared that the Ronson ship's designer had used similar geometric principles but had used different fractions in his equations to determine the lengths of his straight lines and the centers and radii of his sweeps.

Since the Ronson ship's cross sections appeared to be designed using a geometric system, George Matson, a retired naval architect who spent many days analyzing the ship's hull, wondered if the shape and size of the rabbet in the stem were also as described by Bushnell and Deane. They drew their stem rabbets as one large arc that met the keel and continued up approximately ninety degrees to vertical. Since our stem was undergoing conservation treatment at the time, George and I rolled out the fourteen-foot 1:1 tracing of the stem onto the Mariners' Museum patio and found that the stem rabbet described approximately ninety degrees of a sixteen-foot arc. In addition, though the seventeenth-century shipwrights did not suggest doing so, we found that the breast hook, which horizontally crossed the stem to tie both sides of the bow together, described a horizontal eight-foot arc where it lay against the bow frames. Both the bow and breast hook sweeps were precise to within one eighth of an inch. We then decided that indeed, the Ronson ship's architect had used a geometric method similar to Bushnell's and Deane's to determine the hull's shape, but had used different fractions to design a different type of ship. Discovering what those fractions were, and how he used them, would take two summers of *lock the door, don't answer the phone* immersion in the data to "get into the shipwright's mind," as Dick Steffy would have said.

A colleague's question about the average registered tonnage of merchant ships in colonial port records sparked a simple solution to our ship's designed tonnage. The average I quoted to him was 94 tons, yet

I cautioned him that in the records the tonnage was almost always rounded to the nearest 10 tons. Then it occurred to me that the eighteenth-century merchant ordering our ship probably would have done the same, ordering a 200-ton (London formula) capacity ship, not one of 198 tons. This realization would be important when analyzing the design.

Using the dimensions of our ship, I drafted a quick plan of a 200-ton ship as designed by Bushnell and another by Deane. George Matson and Walter Wales had done the latter before for me, but unfortunately with some of the initial, incorrect data I had given them. Neither of my new drawings fitted the ship we had excavated. To determine the pattern of fractions used in the design I wrote a simple computer program, but to do so I shifted the measurements into their decimal equivalents. I soon realized it was a waste of time as the shipwright was most likely thinking in feet and inches, or fractions thereof. Working backward in decimal equivalents did not show any obvious pattern.

I then shifted back to British feet and inches and tried different combinations, with more and less complex fractions of the ship's maximum breadth and keel length for the arcs. As I tried different variations using modern versions of eighteenth-century drafting tools, it slowly became clear to me that when I used simpler fractions the arcs fitted better, especially when using fractions of the ship's maximum breadth (B) of 24 feet instead of the keel length. One day I realized that one of the arcs in the ship's midship cross section was a

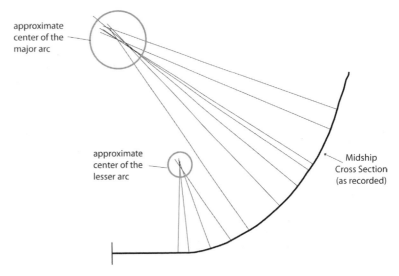

Testing the shipwright's use of arcs on the Ronson ship's midships cross section. *Illustration by Warren Riess.*

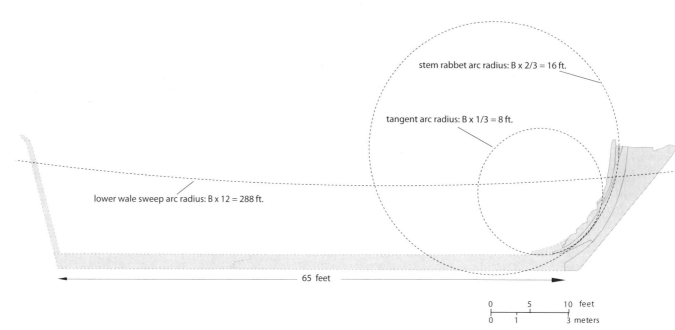

stem rabbet arc radius: B x 2/3 = 16 ft.

tangent arc radius: B x 1/3 = 8 ft.

lower wale sweep arc radius: B x 12 = 288 ft.

65 feet

| 0 | 5 | 10 feet |

| 0 | 1 | 3 meters |

Basic lines of the shipwright's design, based on straight lines and arc radii that were simple fractions or multiples of 24 feet, the ship's maximum breadth (B). *Illustration by Warren Riess.*

perfect 12 feet, or ½ B. Could it be that simple? Within three days I drew various key cross sections and side views that matched the constructed hull shape well for the cargo hold using nothing but straight lines and arcs with radii of 4, 8, 12, and 16 feet. While I was doing so I remembered the stem rabbet and breast hook George Matson and I had discovered years before of 8 and 16 feet (or ⅓ and ⅔ B). Also, the ship's depth of hold was exactly 9 feet (⅜ B).

The shipwright had kept the whole design as simple as possible. As a base for his design he had used a maximum breadth of 24, a number from which one can generate several whole numbers that are simple fractions: 2, 3, 4, 6, 8, 9, 12, 15, 16, and 18. After these realizations I returned to my "ancient" tools and designed the entire hull, I believe the same way the original designer did approximately three hundred years ago, using simple fractions and multiples of the designed maximum breadth, to determine all of the straight lines as well as positions and radii of every arc in the ship. This simple design technique, heretofore unknown by modern scholars, appears to produce the best fit with the ship we had excavated.

SOME REFLECTIONS ON THE SHIP'S DESIGN

The fact that the Manhattan ship was designed to incorporate square, rather than cant, frames reflects

the continuation of an earlier ship design tradition. Whereas surviving treatises and other archaeological remains indicate that eighteenth-century *warship* architects had switched to using cant frames in the bow, the designer of this merchantman continued to use square frames for the bow. It is not clear whether this was because of strictly traditional forces or because the availability of greater amounts of timber in America made square frames more practical for this ship.

Remains of the Ronson ship are additional evidence that the geometric method of ship design was used throughout the period since Bushnell and Deane published the geometric method in 1669 and 1670, the Ronson ship was constructed in the early 1700s, and Sutherland and Murray described the same method in 1726 and 1754. Because this ship's designer, Bushnell, and Deane each provided different radii fractions for the geometric method, and Sutherland and Murray recorded no fractions for the technique, the only three sources imply that various proportions were used for different ships. However, one must be cautious about conclusions based on two treatises and only one physical example.

Though surviving treatises indicated that the geometric method was used to design warships of the period, the Ronson ship's remains are the first indication that eighteenth-century merchant ships were also designed by this method. The use of fractions that were much simpler than those used by Bushnell or Deane probably reflects some of the differences between warships and merchantmen at that time. The shape of the ship, which appears to be a successful combination of the British frigate and Dutch flyboat, suggests an answer to some questions about the means by which British shipwrights developed more efficient merchantmen as they helped the empire expand in the early eighteenth century. However, generalizing further about major trends in ship design is not appropriate, for this ship is only one example. One must keep in mind that we do not know if the vessel was a typical British merchant ship of the early eighteenth century or one of a kind. We now know how this ship was designed and built, but I have found no indication that it was a common type or anomalous. To develop further hypotheses we must await the discovery and study of other transoceanic merchant ships from that period.

CHAPTER SIX

Identifying
the Ship

A SHIP WITH NO NAME, and therefore no history, would limit the interpretation of the archaeological data to a generic merchant ship of the early eighteenth century. By narrowing the vessel's identity I hoped to construct a more accurate micro-history of parts of the British Empire within a specific time period. Because the Ronson ship was the largest object used for fill in the 175 Water Street block, one might assume that the use of the ship would have been newsworthy, and that the event of placing the hull in position would have been recorded in local newspapers, city records, and private financial records. The name of the ship might even be remembered in local lore. However, the identity of the ship was not immediately available from the historical data about the city block, possibly because the use of derelict ships for cribbing was too common in the eighteenth century. Therefore, while analyzing the shipwright's construction and design method I commenced research to determine indirectly the name of the vessel, or at least its origin and uses.

My strategy to identify the ship was to employ four research methods: a consideration of the morphology (shape and size) of the ship's structure, a biological analysis of the timber and shipworms left in the wood, an archaeological analysis of the artifacts and fill found in the hull, and a historical investigation of available records. Some of the methodology was only within the ken of professional experts in other disciplines, such as naval architects and wood and shipworm biologists. Their work helped guide my more traditional historical and archaeological inquiry. I decided to conduct all four exercises because of the relative obscurity of the ship's identity and the synergistic effect of gathering data through four disciplines. Information from

each method provided both direction for research in the other three methods and the elimination of certain possibilities that might otherwise have led the research down long dead-end paths.

MORPHOLOGY OF THE SHIP

Morphological research involves the determination of a subject's shape and size and a comparison of such characteristics with those of other known subjects. In the case of the Ronson ship I could use for such comparisons the general shape and size of the hull; the presence, position, and size of certain features and hardware; and the specific dimensions of certain timbers to determine the measuring system used by the builders. These characteristics might help determine the nationality of the designer and builder, the intended use of the ship when she was built, and the areas of the world to which she sailed.

The ship remains that we excavated in the mud in 1982 were far different from the vessel that was launched sometime in the early eighteenth century. Evidence of damage and repairs to the interior of the hull, including the addition of a second foremast step over a damaged one, as well as shipworm damage to some hull planking and timbers, indicate that the vessel served a rigorous life. Years at sea tended to change the shape of a wooden ship, as its hull shifted and hogged (bow and stern sag) from continued flexing and straining as it moved through ocean waves. In addition, more than 230 years of burial beneath Manhattan caused the vessel's sides to splay (sag outward).

To compare the shape and form of the hull to those of other ships from the same century, I had to determine the ship's original shape. A team of four volunteers at the Mariners' Museum helped us analyze the field data, which consisted of thousands of sketches, charts of measurements, and photographs. During the excavation we recorded the hull in reference to a horizontal plane, but the ship was listing to port (tilting to the left) about three degrees, it was down at the bow about three degrees, and some of our critical data had been destroyed as we left the site. It took more than a year to fit all the pieces together into an approximate plan of the ship.

Armed with the approximate dimensions and using Anthony Deane's 1670 published method, George Matson, a retired naval architect in Newport News, drafted a version of the ship as we had found it in New York. He made adjustments for assumed changes after burial, such as collapsed decks, and he faired the lines of the hull.[1] Fairing is a graphic process by which one repeatedly tests various slight adjustments to the hull shape in three views until all the drawn views fit in proof of a workable shape. It is a long, laborious process that can only be conducted by a trained, patient specialist. After adding construction details, Matson was able to offer a good estimate of the ship, based on Deane, long before I determined that the shipwright actually designed it using a different method.

Despite the trouble with the data in determining the ship's exact dimensions, my research could proceed, based on rough proportions. When launched, the Ronson ship was 82 feet long between perpendiculars (measured from the inside top of the stem to the inside top of the stern post), or approximately 100 feet overall, with a keel approximately 65 feet long. She had a maximum breadth of 24 feet, a 9-foot-deep cargo hold, and drew approximately 11 feet of water when fully loaded.

When merchant ships were registered and leased, a standard way of describing their capacity was needed. The capacity figure developed was called *tonnage,* which at that time was a volume, rather than a weight measurement, with one ton equal to approximately forty cubic feet. The formula for deriving a ship's tonnage was different in each country and colony and has changed through the centuries. However, even when historical documents indicate that a particular formula should have been used at a particular port and year, we find differences in the archives of registered tonnage for the same ship. It was a way to approximate, rather than exactly calculate, the spatial capacity of a ship.

When we compare archaeological remains to the recorded tonnage of particular ships we see more discrepancies. Everything indicates that the people who used the formulae to define a ship's tonnage used them only as rough guides. According to a common early 1700s British formula of length of keel x maximum breadth x ½ maximum breadth ÷ 94 = tonnage, the ship we excavated would have had a measured tonnage of approximately 200 tons.[2] Americans often replaced "½ maximum breadth" with "depth of cargo hold," which in our ship was 9 feet, rather than 12 feet. Therefore an American merchantman of these same dimensions might have been registered in London at 200 tons, or in one of the colonial ports at or below 150 tons.[3]

The overall shape and size of the ship at 175 Water Street indicate that she was a larger than average merchantman, though not as large as the great East Indiamen, which were typically registered at 600 tons. There is substantial evidence that identifies the vessel as a merchant ship, rather than a warship. For example, a warship of this size would have had more than four small gunports on the lower deck; in fact, the lower deck would have been the gun deck. The Ronson ship's gunports were proportioned specifically and just the right height above the deck for six-pounder cannon, which shot six-pound cast-iron balls. The gunports on an eighteenth-century warship of this size would have been designed for guns larger than six-pounders, and more support knees would have braced the deck beams to carry the weight of many heavier guns.

Other features that the Ronson ship shared with merchantmen were a complete run of caulked ceiling planks, a similar placement of the hawse holes, a windlass, and a lack of compartmentalization below decks. Caulked ceiling planks stiffened the hull against hogging and protected the cargo from moisture condensed on the inside of the outer planking. In contrast, a warship generally had intermittent ceiling strakes to facilitate maintenance and repairs to the hull. On this ship the hawse holes, which let the anchor cables into the bow, were above the upper deck, rather than between the two decks as on a warship. In addition, the Ronson ship had a windlass (a large horizontal winch), a feature of eighteenth-century merchantmen but not of warships of the period.[4] In the areas of the ship that were still in existence when we excavated it, most other differences between a merchant and warship would have involved the ship's hardware and cargo, all of which had been stripped from the ship before it was buried.

To determine the type of merchant ship, I compared the vessel's shape to those in eighteenth-century plans, drawings, and paintings. Before the mid-eighteenth century, merchant ships were generally classified by their hull type rather than as today, when their sail and mast configuration determines the class of vessel. For example, *bark* in 1750 was the name given to a type of hull. A few years later, bark referred to a particular mast and sail type. In 1768 Fredrik Chapman, one of the leading shipwrights of his time, published *Architectura Navalis Mercatoria*, a treatise on ship design.[5] Chapman followed his father's trade by apprenticing to the Swedish Navy Dockyard in 1738. By his retirement in 1793, he had worked in England, France, Holland, and Sweden, eventually becoming the vice admiral in charge of Swedish naval shipbuilding. During his lifetime he collected his own and others' drafts of ships and small craft of the Western world. His collection is now held by the Swedish Maritime Museum.[6]

The Ronson ship fits Chapman's description of a *merchant frigate*, except for its midship area, which is more like that of Chapman's *bark* or *flyboat*. The relatively flat bottom in the middle of the Ronson ship would give it a shallower draft per ton than a typical merchant frigate shown in Chapman's treatise.[7]

Though the term *frigate* refers only to a warship today, in the eighteenth century it also referred to a class of merchant ships. Merchant frigates were sturdy transoceanic ships that could be heavily armed to protect valuable cargo. They were generally good sailing vessels, but they required more crew than other vessels of a similar size in order to work the sails in foul weather and the greater number of guns in a fight. This was a drawback, since wages, food, and water for the crew were an important part of the cost of running merchant vessels. The extra men, and supplies needed for them, also took space that could otherwise be used to carry cargo. Therefore a large crew meant an expensive ship to run. However, the number of sails used on a ship was determined by the number of men available to work the large square canvases. With their larger crews, frigates could carry more sail than other merchant ships. More sails per size of ship equaled more power to sustain speed at sea. Thus a frigate was generally faster as well as stronger than other merchant ships.

For their length and breadth merchant frigates were not the most spacious of cargo vessels. Their efficiency, both in cargo capacity and number of crew per ton of cargo, was lower than that of ships sailing with less protection aboard.[8] The decreased cargo capacity and increased crew meant a relatively high cost per unit of cargo transported. Therefore I inferred from its size and general shape that the Ronson ship was designed to carry a valuable or important cargo to or from shallow waters, along a route where trouble was expected.

Since merchant ships were built along similar lines in most of the northern European countries and some of their colonies, sometimes it is difficult to determine the nationality of a ship by considering its general shape. Shipwrights and shipbuilding ideas moved from one country to another, and ships of the same size built in the same shipyard varied in shape depending on their intended use, their owners' ideas of a good ship, and the sailing qualities of the last ship built there. In northern Europe, shallow draft ships were most common in Holland, where the ships had to navigate shifting sand bars to use Dutch ports. However, shallow draft ships were also used in other areas of the world, such as the northern coal ports of England and the Chesapeake Bay in America.[9]

To find ships with similar shapes I inspected Chapman's unpublished ship draft collection. No ship in Chapman's collection stands out as being most like the Ronson ship, but three ship types had elements in common with it. Although shorter in length and smaller in draft, the Ronson ship had the general appearance of Chapman's English West Indies trader. Below the waterline the Ronson ship had a flatter bottom and sharper turn-of-the-bilge (an abrupt turn up to the side) than Chapman's English ship. The bottom and turn-of-the-bilge were more like those of the French and Dutch flyboats, which were designed for carrying maximum cargo in shallow friendly waters. However, the stern of the Ronson ship looked like a square tucked stern, used more by the British but also by the French and Dutch to a lesser extent. The general shape of the Ronson ship, therefore, suggested a British merchantman that was modified to carry more cargo into shallow waters.[10]

In order to identify more accurately the nationality of the ship I took a close look at some of the vessel's construction details. Identifying the origin of the Ronson ship by a comparison of construction details is difficult, because again there are only a few examples of detailed ship plans for the period, and as far as I can determine from the surviving archival and archaeological data, construction traditions were not necessarily different in each location. For example, the frame pattern on the Ronson ship appears to be consistent with existing plans of other ships from various countries. This shipwright joined the outer hull planks with simple diagonal scarf joints, three times as long as the timbers' widths. Diagonal scarfs of these dimensions appear to be common to many shipbuilding traditions.[11]

Just inside the gunwales (upper sides of the vessel), along the outside edge of the lower deck, the waterways were a distinct shape throughout the length of the ship. The vessel's waterways were horizontal planks, three inches thick by six inches wide, which served as both the outermost deck plank and a ceiling (inside hull) plank at the intersection of the deck and ceiling. The shape of the Ronson ship waterways was similar to those on the seventy-four-gun HMS *Bellona,* launched in Chatham, England in 1760, and the Dutch East Indiaman *Noordt Nieuw Landt,* built in Rotterdam in 1750.[12] Two French examples from the eighteenth century show a distinctively different style of waterway, which forms a forty-five-degree angle at the intersection of deck and ceiling.[13] These examples, however, were slim evidence to support any hypothesis about our ship's origin, especially since only one of the five examples was a merchantman.

In a parallel study, I tried to determine the measuring system of the ship builder. Measuring systems within each country or empire were standardized only late in the eighteenth century. I hoped that establishing the system used on the Ronson ship would shed light on the country of origin. During the archaeological excavation in 1982 all measurements were taken in the British standard to a precision of one quarter of an inch. Only the knightshead, a vertical bitt or securing post in the bow, seemed to be made using exact British inches. To determine the original measuring system I used a system different from any of the supposed possibilities—namely the metric system, first adopted in Europe well after the Ronson ship had been built—to measure a number of timbers again. Then I sought a common denominator for the measurements and compared that common denominator to the known eighteenth-century scales to see if one matched.

After measuring many aspects of the timbers and analyzing hundreds of filed measurements, I realized that in the eighteenth century, finishing ship timbers and overall dimensions to within an inch on a ship was not important to the builder. For example, the draft marks on the Ronson ship's stem, which allowed the

master to know how deep the vessel sat in the water, were approximately one foot apart, but the distances between marks varied from 10¼ to 13¼ inches. A similar variation of draft marks was noted on remains of a Swedish ship that wrecked in 1730.[14] The distance between deck beams varied from 37 inches to 53 inches.

There are two locations on the ship where one might expect the shipwright to have taken particular care to fashion pieces precisely in order to have two pieces fit together properly: the dovetails where the deck beams fastened to the side of the ship, and the hatch coaming on which the cargo hatches rested. Unfortunately, after the hatch coamings had been measured and mapped carefully in the British system and photographed in the field, the coamings had been discarded due to time constraints on the site. They could not be used for the study. Each of the existing deck beam dovetail joints is a slightly different size and shape, with adze marks on the surface. It appears that the open or female sides of the dovetails, in the sides of the ship, were carved with an adze to an approximate size and shape, and their male counterparts on the deck beams were then individually carved to match each, evidently without being measured with a rule. Thus none of the most probable places yielded information about the measuring system used by the builder. Only the knightshead in the bow, seemingly made to the British system, remained a clue.

Then, in 1986, evidence of the builder's measuring system came by surprise when I was studying the design technique used by the ship's architect. George Matson and I discovered that the stem rabbet, a groove in the stem that accepted the forward end of outer planks, described an arc with a radius of 16 feet, 0 inches in the British system. Perpendicular to the stem and inside it was a series of three breast hooks—large timbers that held the two sides of the bow together. Two were made of three pieces of wood, but the third was made of a single curved timber. The outside edge of the single-timber breast hook described an arc with a radius of 8 feet, 0 inches in the British system. Both measurements were precise to an eighth of an inch. At first I thought these two figures indicated that the ship was built in the British Empire, but the two measurements are also divisible by the eighteenth-century French and Antwerp foot. The two radii equaled exactly 15 feet, 0 inches and 7 feet, 6 inches respectively in France, and 17 feet, 0 inches and 8 feet, 6 inches in Antwerp.[15] Thus, by considering the

A 1717 engraving of New York's East River showing what appears to be a storage hulk along the quay. Detail from *A view of New York from Brooklyn Heights* (William Burgis, c. 1717). *Collection of the New-York Historical Society, image 32098.*

measuring system I narrowed the ship's construction to three nationalities, but the knightshead's dimensions weighted the argument toward the British.

In a third course of analysis I examined the hull remains to determine the ship's age. I found physical evidence that she was abandoned because of age, use, and possibly accidental damage. No charred timbers or other indications suggested that the ship was even partially burned. However, the remains did show evidence of a number of repairs. The foremast step, which held the forward of three masts, had split and was crudely covered by a new step. The amidships waterway had been split and repaired. Damage to the outer planking indicated that the one-inch-thick outer sheathing, usually replaced every few years, had been replaced at least once. Probably because of earlier damage to the sheathing, shipworms had found their way through the sheathing, hair, and pitch to colonize some of the outer planking and the stem itself. Damage to the oak planking had been caulked and covered again with pitch and sheathing.

The repairs indicated that the ship served for a few years as a sailing merchantman before being either abandoned or used as a moored hulk. Colonial merchantmen had an average life span of approximately eight years.[16] Ships that could not be sailed anymore

were often used as floating warehouses and sometimes as retail venues in harbors. If used as a storage hulk, like some of the ships in the 1717 Burgis view of New York, the Ronson ship may have remained afloat for a number of years before being placed parallel to the shore to crib fill.

ARTIFACT ANALYSIS

Although only a few of the artifacts found in the ship are considered to be associated with the ship during her sailing life, I felt that an analysis of all the artifacts might help lead me to the ship's identity. Artifacts found in the bottom of the hull, and in fairly inaccessible areas of the hull, were likely associated with the vessel's life and might indicate the origin and uses of the ship. A study of the fill, placed in the hull when it was positioned to crib fill in New York, could conceivably allow us to date the burying of the hull and might thereby direct my archival research to a particular time slot.

Unfortunately, most of the artifacts that were probably associated with the ship's life are not definitely assignable to a country or time period, within a few decades. Two wooden buckets, a leather armlet, a leather protective mask, and a nautical pulley block are all artifact types that have been associated with several countries throughout the 1700s. An intact spirits bottle, found in the stern under the cabin, may relate to the life of the ship. It is associated with English sites from 1720 to 1757.[17] Clay pipe sherds found in the lowest layer within the ship, which therefore may be associated with the final voyage ballast of the ship (see chapter 8), were made in England and date from circa 1720.[18] Although single English bottles might be expected on ships from other countries, the exclusively English style of clay pipe sherds suggested that this was indeed a British ship. Fragments of other artifacts in the bottom layer of fill indicated that the ship may have sailed last in the 1720s.

Artifacts from every layer of fill, except the lowest in the hull, evidently were dumped there with other ships' ballast and local refuse dirt. These artifacts vary in their origin, but were mainly products of the British Empire. Only two artifacts have dates on them: a balance-beam scale lead weight with the year 1746 scratched on its face and a ceramic jug with 1747 molded into a medallion on its neck. The rest of the more than five thousand artifacts found in the upper layers of fill have manufacturing date ranges from 1670 to 1770, with a graphed peak date in the 1740s. The 1760–70 artifacts were in the very top layer, suggesting that they were left there after the ship had been interred.

Although the artifacts from all the layers cannot identify the origin of the ship, their type and date ranges indicate that the ship probably sailed with a British crew until sometime in the 1720s and then was buried in the late 1740s or 1750s, probably the late 1740s. If it had been buried before 1747 some of the artifacts, especially the weight and ceramic jug, would not have been found in the hull. If it were filled after the 1750s the later date of the artifacts probably would have been higher.

BIOLOGICAL ANALYSIS

Biological analysis of the ship's remains is another method of determining the vessel's origin, its intended use, and the actual geographic areas sailed. Although some eighteenth-century shipwrights moved timber great distances before shaping it to form part of a ship, most did not. Therefore the identification of the exact species of woods used on the Ronson ship might indicate the area in which she was built. Certain species of wood were also preferred for specific uses in vessels, such as oak for outer planking. Determining the species of wood used for a specific purpose on the Ronson ship might therefore indicate if certain preferred types of wood were available to the shipwright, possibly indicating something about local economics. In addition, a determination of the species of shipworms in the hull's sheathing might indicate to what geographic areas the ship sailed.

To determine the species of wood used on the Ronson ship we had sent samples of various timbers to three laboratories: the Center for Wood Anatomy Research, United States Forest Products Laboratory; the Forest Products Laboratory, University of Maine; and the Department of Forest Products, Virginia Polytechnic Institute. All three laboratories concluded that because the wood was so degraded, the determination of exact species in most cases would be impossible, but that some information could be extracted.

Wood analysts usually provide species information with degrees of certainty. A stated genus or species, such as "white oak," equals a positive identification. "Probable" and "possible" are terms used to denote

lower degrees of certainty. Each laboratory was given only a limited number of wood samples, with only some samples coming from the same timber. Also, the United States Forest Products Laboratory was sent samples of different trunnels than the trunnels sent to the University of Maine laboratory. Therefore each identified different woods for the trunnels.

The three laboratories found that in general, the main structural timbers, outer planking, and ceiling planking of the ship were made from trees of the white oak group, "possibly" live oak (*Quercus virginiana*). Live oak, so named because it does not lose its old leaves until new spring leaves appear, is part of the white oak group. Trees in that group were once found in many areas of the world, including most coastal areas of North America and northern Europe, but in the eighteenth century live oak was found only in the coastal plains of North America, from southern Virginia to northern Mexico. Live oak is an exceedingly strong and heavy wood, which is rot resistant and is found in a variety of natural curves, making it very useful for curved structural timbers in shipbuilding.[19] From historical records we know that it was used for making ships at least by the 1740s in southern North America and was shipped as material to other shipbuilding areas as early as 1775. In the nineteenth century, shipwrights from New England often sent teams of men south in the winter to acquire a load of live oak for their New England shipyards.[20]

Southern yellow (hard) pine was used for most of the ship's decking, the remaining bilge pump, and at least one of the trunnels. Which species of southern yellow pine was used has not been discernible; there are ten species of southern yellow pine, which are difficult to distinguish from one another when only decomposed wood samples are available. Yellow pine's natural range is from Connecticut to Texas, but it is most plentiful from Virginia to Texas.[21] At least one plank of the deck was made of red pine (*Pinus resinosa*) or scotch pine (*P. sylvestris*). The former is a North American wood that had a natural range from Canada to Maryland, while the latter is from the British Isles. Unfortunately, they cannot be distinguished from each other when the wood is degraded.

When we cut the margin strake (outermost deck plank) during excavation we noted that the sawdust was pink, and a pungent cedar smell arose. We concluded that the margin strake was made of juniper, or red cedar (*Juniperus* sp), but no samples were sent to a laboratory for microscopic identification. Juniper is rot resistant, making it a good wood for a margin strake, on which rainwater might collect. In North America several species of juniper are found from Maine to Texas.[22]

A sample of sixty-one trunnels was sent for identification. Of these, fifty-five were oak (possibly a mixture of various species of oak), two were eastern white pine (*Pinus strobus*), and there was one trunnel each of southern yellow pine, ash (*Fraxinus* sp.), hickory (*Carya* sp.), and juniper (*Juniperus* sp.). Since eighteenth-century British instructions for trunnels usually required them to be made of oak, we were surprised to find so many species used on this ship. Although ash, hickory, yellow pine, and juniper might be suitable substitutes for oak trunnels, white pine would seem to be too weak to hold the ship together. The white pine, or all of the non-oak trunnels, may have been expedient replacements for loose trunnels during a voyage. Ash trunnels could be carved from a broken oar, hickory from a tool handle, yellow pine from a deck plank, juniper from a margin strake, and white pine from a rigging spar. Most of the trunnel species are found in both America and Europe, but hickory is native only to North America.

The mizzen (aft) mast was made of white pine, a North American wood prized for its outstanding usefulness for ship masts and spars. The main spindle of the capstan (a vertical, hand-powered winch), which appears to have been added to the ship after its sailing days, was made of elm, a hardwood found on both sides of the Atlantic Ocean. The capstan's whelps (brackets around which the rope was wound) were made of oak.

In the 1980s few conclusions could be reached from the botanical information alone. The wood's degraded state made it impossible to distinguish exactly which species had been used for the main timbers of the ship. Although many "probable" and "possible" identifications suggested that the ship had been made of American woods, they did not prove it. If the probable and possible identifications were accurate, the vessel was built mostly of live oak, with decks mainly of southern yellow pine. Live oak is limited to the southern coastal plain of North America, and there is no information indicating that large amounts of live oak were transported out of the area for shipbuilding in the early eighteenth century.[23] Therefore the botanical evidence suggested, but did not prove, that the Ronson ship was built in the southern North American

colonies—Virginia, North Carolina, or South Carolina. Georgia was not a colony until later.

Not discouraged, I hoped that future scientific advances would eventually provide the means to determine an exact species of oak. For the rest of my research and identification arguments I decided to use the probable live oak identification as a guide, but always with the stated understanding that the species identification was not definite. I also kept my eyes open in the archives for data that might be useful if the wood was eventually identified as another species of oak. It was not until 2010 that the Mariners' Museum and I received a definitive species identification from Dr. Robert Blanchette of the University of Minnesota. He used a scanning electron microscope to determine positively that the two largest timbers in the bow, the stem and the single-timber breast hook, were made of live oak. His report removed a major weight from my mind, as it meant that I had not spent years of research on an incorrect path.

Another biological investigation was made, of the shipworm remains found in the outer sheathing of the hull. Shipworms are not really worms but bivalves that invade dead wood during their free-swimming larval period. A larva makes only a small hole when it enters the wood, and the opening remains quite small thereafter, even while the animal enlarges its tunnel as it grows. Thus, when it dies, calcium-based parts of the shipworm remain trapped inside the tunnel. These remains can be used to identify the species of shipworm, even when the animal has been dead for more than 230 years.[24]

During the excavation we asked Avery Stone, a friend from a former archaeological shipwreck investigation, to take a sample of the Ronson ship's outer sheathing to Dr. Ruth Turner, the world's authority on shipworms, at the Museum of Comparative Zoology at Harvard. She identified three species of shipworms: *Teredo mindanensis*, *Bankia carinata*, and *B. campanullata*. The native habitat of *Teredo mindanensis* is the coast of the Pacific islands, Southeast Asia, Indonesia, New Guinea, and the Philippines. *Bankia carinata* is found in tropical waters around the world but primarily from the Mediterranean to the Caribbean. *Bankia campanullata* is found on the east coast of South America and throughout the Indian Ocean.[25]

At first glance, this information might indicate that the Ronson ship sailed throughout the world. However, the ship need not have visited any of the above places to pick up these three species of shipworms. Ship-worms typically spawn in warm summer waters, and most shipworms in a harbor or bay, even different species, will spawn at the same time. Each species tends to compete better in different circumstances of water temperature, salinity, available wood species, and other factors. If another ship picked up *Teredo mindanensis* in the Philippines and was riding at anchor in a warm port elsewhere during spawning time for the species, the shipworm larvae could seek out the nearest dead wood and enter it. That wood could be the sheathing of another ship at anchor nearby. This scenario was probably common during the eighteenth century because during peace and war, merchantmen and warships from the British, Spanish, Dutch, and French empires often called at the same ports as naval vessels, merchantmen, or prizes of war.[26]

Thus our ship could have picked up all three species in one port at the same time, from other ships anchored near it. Since the outer sheathing was typically replaced every few years, the event would have taken place in its last years of sailing. The three species of shipworms spawn only in warm waters, not in northern ports like New York or the British Isles. Thus the zoological investigation of the ship's parasitic shipworms suggested that the Ronson ship was in a warm water port, with vessels from various regions of the world, during her last years under sail. The fact that no species of shipworm natural to North American waters was found does not eliminate this ship from having been built or sailed in a British American colony. It only means that the ship was not in American saline areas when the shipworms were spawning. Experienced captains in Chesapeake Bay typically moved their ships up the rivers to fresh water during spawning time to prevent the shipworm larvae from boring into their wooden sheathing.

ARCHIVAL RESEARCH

Morphological, archaeological, and biological evidence provided some direction for historical research of the Ronson ship. Measurements on the knightshead, stem, and breast hook indicated that the ship was built to the eighteenth-century foot of Antwerp, France, or the British Empire, more likely the latter. Her shape, especially that of the stern, and her size indicated that she was an ocean-sailing British merchant frigate, designed to carry valuable cargoes in shallow

waters where danger was anticipated. The three botanical studies of her timbers in the 1980s strongly suggested, but did not prove, that the ship was built in Virginia or the Carolinas. The zoological study and evidence of repairs and maintenance implied that the ship was in a warm water port outside North America during the last few years of her sailing career. Finally, analysis of the artifacts from within the hull suggested that the ship last sailed in the 1720s with a British crew and was buried between 1747 and 1760.

The ship's position in the 175 Water Street block also provided some clues for further research. The hull lay roughly parallel to the eighteenth-century shoreline, where the water had been approximately eight feet deep at high tide. Dr. Amy Friedlander had identified the original owners of the block, and had garnered some information about them, when she researched the block's history for the project before archaeologists discovered the ship. I felt that a new inspection of information about the owners who filled out over the water might shed light on the identification of the ship. However, neither Amy nor I found any mention in surviving records of a ship placed in the water lots.[27]

Not finding evidence of the ship in the water lot owners' records, I began a study of other New York records in the first half of the eighteenth century, a determination of which accessible ports required shallow draft ships, and a review of related records from those ports. These studies were meant to isolate ships fitting the physical evidence at hand; the individual ships could then be investigated to see if one matched the ship at 175 Water Street. Archival materials for the colonial period are meager. Few records exist for anything except noted people and their relevant interests. Lists and records of common enterprises, such as shipping and trade, were generally not deemed worthy of saving for future generations. Even some official shipping records, intended for safekeeping, were purposely or accidentally destroyed in later years. Thus finding references and especially details about specific ships and individuals is often a frustrating, fruitless endeavor. However, some records do exist. Pertinent surviving eighteenth-century colonial New York records include various maps of the city and some of the Naval Office Shipping Lists, customs records, the *New York Gazette and Weekly Post Boy*, Prize Court proceedings, and merchants' records.

Surviving eighteenth-century maps of Manhattan indicate that the eastern half of the 175 Water Street block was filled between 1744 and 1755.[28] This information reinforced and refined the artifact analysis dates of 1747 to 1760, to provide a burial date between 1747 and 1755.

Each colony's clerk of the Naval Office, often called the naval officer though he was not part of the navy, compiled for the crown the Naval Office Shipping Lists (NOSLs). The NOSLs included much information about each merchant ship that entered or cleared the colonial ports. Each naval clerk recorded the information slightly differently, but in most cases they recorded the date, ship name, ship home port, name of the master (captain), type of vessel, tons, number of guns (cannon), number of men, when and where built, when and where registered, principal owner, a list of the cargo, the port it was coming from or going to, and where and when it was last bonded (to obey the British trade laws). Four times a year the clerk sent a copy to London, where clerks would follow all the British merchant ships' voyages to make certain each was only in ports where it should be trading, carrying only legal goods, and paying necessary fees.

Many of the NOSLs did not survive 230 years of storage. For New York the records generally survived from 1715 to the Revolutionary War, but some pertinent periods are missing, including the critical times for our ship from April 1743 to April 1748 and September 1748 to 1751.[29] My study of all merchant ships registered at 100 tons or more listed in the New York NOSLs from 1715 through 1748 identified some ships that were listed as entering the port but not clearing from it. Unfortunately, since the records have gaps as much as five years long, many ships departed and entered New York without being noted in the existing NOSLs.

To acquire more data for the period and especially to cover the intervals with no NOSLs, I organized a team of volunteer readers at the Mariners' Museum to study microfilms of all the existing New York Gazette and Weekly Post Boy issues from January 2, 1732, to 1759. The New York Gazette, which became the New York Weekly Post Boy, was a weekly newspaper, usually four pages long. One of its regular short columns was the list of the names of ships entering and clearing the port, and it included other scattered information about some of the vessels, merchants, and general events in the port. Once again there are large gaps in the existing newspapers. For some periods neither the NOSLs nor the newspapers exist. Combining information from the New York Gazette and Weekly Post Boy and the NOSLs revealed a number of ships that could be the Ronson

ship, but no ship stood out as the obvious choice.[30] Several ships came into New York between 1725 and 1755 that were between 100 and 250 tons and were built in the southern colonies, but the existing records indicate that all of them left the port. I could not determine whether those or other ships entered the port during the breaks in the existing records and never left.

By process of elimination, I thought for quite some time that the Ronson ship was probably built in Virginia, where the major export in the early eighteenth century was tobacco. In the late seventeenth and early eighteenth centuries many English shipwrights emigrated to the Chesapeake to build ships for the rapidly expanding merchant fleet of the empire.[31] Although Maryland also bordered the Chesapeake, live oak's northernmost natural habitat was in Virginia—not across the bay in Maryland. In a study parallel to that for New York, I extracted and analyzed similar information from the other colonial port records through December 1752, looking for clues about Virginia-built ships that disappeared at the proper time or that also appeared in the New York port records or the New York Gazette and Weekly Post Boy. I was happy to find that several ships were the proper size and built between 1700 and 1740—one of them was sure to be the ship I was studying.

Scrutinizing the available records for each possible Virginia-built ship, I eventually narrowed the field to two possibilities: Sarah and Mary and Mortimer. The two-hundred-ton Sarah and Mary was built in Virginia in 1726 for London owners. She carried tobacco and forest products to London between 1727 and 1733 and returned each time with various "European goods." The last record I found for Sarah and Mary was for her sailing from Yorktown, Virginia, for London in July 1733. Mortimer, another Virginia-built ship of 200 tons, also was a candidate. Built in 1712, Mortimer yearly carried tobacco and forest products to Bristol, England, and returned with manufactured goods. The last located records certify Mortimer leaving Yorktown for Bristol in September 1746. The New York records indicate that a number of ships from other colonies entered for repairs on their way to England and other eastern ports. Either of the ships could have suffered damage from a storm or accident on its way to England, sailed into New York for repairs, and been condemned as not worth repairing and used as a warehouse or for part of a new quay along the waterfront. I found no evidence to support either of these two ships ever entering New York Harbor. Given all the voids in the port records, I did not see that as a major problem, yet I did not feel the evidence was strong enough to name these two ships as the best possibilities.

Sarah and Mary and *Mortimer* remained on my possible list until in 1993, when while reorganizing my files, I reconsidered all the data collected, beginning with Dr. Turner's study of the shipworm remains. The Ronson ship's hull had three warm water species of shipworms, but no Chesapeake shipworms, in her outer sheathing. The limited records I had for these two ships indicate that their only warm water port was the Chesapeake and that they were both in the Chesapeake during shipworm spawning season. True, each captain could have sailed his ship into fresh water within the Chesapeake at those times to prevent shipworm infestation. However, for these ships to have become infested with other warm water shipworm species while not attracting Chesapeake shipworms at the same time, they would have to have been in another warm water port, far from the Chesapeake, and with no Chesapeake ships nearby during shipworm spawning season. I therefore shelved the *Sarah and Mary* and *Mortimer* files along with all the rest from Virginia, each for a similar reason.

Other than Virginia, the only two British colonies that possessed live oak for the ship were North Carolina and South Carolina. According to Converse Clowse's study of southern shipbuilding, only one ship in either of the Carolinas could have been the Ronson ship—*Princess Carolina*, a 150-ton merchant ship built in 1717 in Charleston, South Carolina. All the other ships built in North or South Carolina before 1740 were smaller than 120 tons.[32] In the various port lists I found records of *Princess Carolina* from 1717 until late in 1728, sometimes listed in London as 200 tons. My research on this ship was concurrent with my research on the Virginia-built merchantmen, yet it remained on my most-likely list as each of the other ships was dropped for one or more reasons.

In the colonial American and London port records I had found that *Princess Carolina* visited New York and left in 1725, but she last appeared in the surviving port records arriving in Virginia from London and Madeira on November 12, 1728.[33] In 1736 the British Admiralty issued a pass (for merchant ships traveling through dangerous areas) to a *Princess Carolina,* but it was a different ship. The latter was a new and smaller ship used for slaving between Gambia and Charleston.[34]

Since the ship's dates and life span fitted, I carefully reconsidered the evidence for *Princess Carolina* being the Ronson ship. Morphological evidence fitted quite well. Our calculated tonnage figure for the Ronson ship measurements was 199 tons (London formula), rounded to 200 tons, which is what I had found for *Princess Carolina*'s registered tonnage when in London. The shape of the Ronson ship hull was also what one might expect for a Charleston-built merchantman. Like the Netherlands ports, Charleston's harbor entrance was guarded by shifting sand bars that hampered large transoceanic ships. An eighteenth-century Charleston ship might well have had the bow and stern of a typical English merchant frigate and a flat-bottomed, shallow draft midsection to allow easier passage over the sandbar that guarded Charleston Harbor.

Also, though I had not considered it earlier, when reviewing my research I noted that *Princess Carolina* was listed a few times in the port records as having four cannon, one of few ships of that size having four cannon. The ship we excavated had four gunports. The naval clerks also occasionally listed the vessels' type of stern. When they did, they noted a "square" stern for *Princess Carolina,* another match with the hull in New York, though square sterns were common.

Another connection provides a possible explanation for *Princess Carolina* entering New York Harbor one last time. A British Navy captain in England wrote to the Admiralty stating that *Princess Carolina* had been in a storm two weeks after sailing from Virginia in 1729, was missing the next day, and was presumed lost. It is possible that the ship survived, the crew made some repairs at sea—such as adding the second foremast step we had found crudely attached—and they sailed west into New York. However, this remains a hypothetical reason for the ship's last return to Manhattan.[35]

The species of wood identified on the Ronson ship closely matched those used to build *Princess Carolina*. South Carolina is well within the natural range of most of the woods found on the ship, including live oak and yellow pine. Some of the oak planks and pine might have been from farther north, but that was going to have to remain a mystery for a while.

More convincing for the *Princess Carolina* identification were the species of shipworms found in the Ronson ship's outer sheathing. The three identified shipworm species were *Teredo mindanensis* (primarily found in the Pacific islands, Southeast Asia, Indonesia, New Guinea, and the Philippines), *Bankia carinata* (found in tropical waters around the world but primarily from the Mediterranean to the Caribbean), and *B. campanullata* (found on the east coast of South America and throughout the Indian Ocean). Few eighteenth-century Atlantic ports would commonly have had ships from all three areas anchored in their harbor at the same time for the Ronson ship to have picked up their larvae during a shipworm spawn. *Princess Carolina* was in three of these ports during the summer spawns: Lisbon, Portugal; Barcelona, Spain; and Funchal on the wine island of Madeira.

Lisbon was a major European port for worldwide trade. East Indiamen, large merchant ships that brought spices and Chinese and Indian goods from the East, would have carried *mindanensis*. They could also carry *campanullata*, as could ships from Brazil laden with sugar and logwood. Ships from the nearby Mediterranean and from Caribbean island colonies would have been riddled with the common *carinata*. There is a good chance that more than one ship from each of these areas was in Lisbon Harbor every summer. *Princess Carolina*'s outer sheathing may have been infested by the shipworms during her stay in Lisbon in the summer of 1725.

The same might be true for the merchant ship's visits to Madeira in 1727 and 1728. Ships from many parts of the world stopped in Madeira for its famous wine and also to replenish stores such as food and water when they were short after a long voyage. Therefore a shipworm spawning in the warm Madeira waters could have infested *Princess Carolina*. All of the above could be said for Barcelona, but I am not sure what months in 1726 *Princess Carolina* was there.

Some important supporting negative evidence can be sifted out of the port records and shipworm identification. Since we found no North American shipworm species in the vessel's outer sheathing, there is a strong probability that the ship was not in an American warm port during the summer months of her last few years of sailing. If she had been, and the captain did not take her into fresh water during shipworm spawning season, we would have found North American species in the sheathing. If the captain had taken the ship to a fresh water area no shipworms would have infested the ship's outer sheathing. The Ronson ship's sheathing was riddled with shipworms, but seemingly none from North America. In the colonial port records I could find, I noted that *Princess Carolina* did not show up in any North American port records for any summer except in June 1727, when she left approximately a week before the normal Chesapeake July shipworm spawn.

Thus the positive and negative shipworm evidence in the Ronson ship's outer sheathing became one of the more convincing arguments for *Princess Carolina* being the ship we excavated in New York. One can never be absolutely sure, but I am quite confident that *Princess Carolina* was the ship we excavated and that I have been studying.

INTRIGUED BY FINDING the ship's probable identity, I began research in records from many locations on the Atlantic Rim to learn more about *Princess Carolina* and those associated with her. In years of research I never found any ship's log, personal diary, or insurance or business records that dealt specifically with the ship in detail. There is strong evidence to indicate that *Princess Carolina* was the Ronson ship, yet I found no document to prove that it was. Also, I found no other ship in the existing port records that could have been the ship we studied in Manhattan. As of today, the Charleston ship remains the vessel that probably was the ship we excavated in New York, but stating that it *definitely* was *Princess Carolina* would be stretching the evidence too far.

Most of the archival material I found about *Princess Carolina* was for her American ports; however, records do exist of some of her arrivals in London and Madeira.

Though most of the eighteenth-century London customs port records were destroyed during World War II, an additional type of record began to be kept in London in 1725. British sailors were required to pay sixpence per month to support Greenwich Hospital, established for disabled sailors. Records were kept, called Ledgers for the Receiver of Sixpenses, that include listings for *Princess Carolina* entering the Thames. Reading through the available port records from South Carolina, New York, Virginia, London, and Madeira I was able to construct an intermittent outline of the ship's life as a merchantman.

Though some serious disclaimers should be kept in mind, presenting the history of the probable ship, without a flawless identification, is a useful exercise to place the excavated ship in its milieu. The story may change as new information is discovered through continued research, but the changes should not be major.

CHAPTER SEVEN

Princess Carolina

Early in 1716 William Wragg and Jonathan Danson were developing a plan. Their conversation may have been something like this:

"We have no choice, Jonathan, but to build our own ship, or South Carolina will not survive," stated Wragg emphatically. "The London-owned vessels are avoiding us because of the dangers here, and they realize better returns carrying Chesapeake tobacco. The colony is faced with ruin without supplies. You must convince the other Lords Proprietors to exempt Master Shipbuilder Austin and his men from military duty in this bloody Indian war. Then Charleston will have its own substantial ship, to serve Charleston's desperate needs."

"Your plan may be our colony's salvation, William, but together we do not have the credit to pay Austin. I am not sure we can raise enough to buy the timber and hardware for the ship. Or perhaps," Danson offered optimistically, "Austin will be willing to accept a part ownership for his pay? The Proprietors meet later this month. I should be able to convince them of the value of this venture for all of Carolina."

"We require more than their blessing," replied Wragg. "Even with their support, the merchants of the port will need to expend almost all of their resources to create and ready the vessel for sea. We also will need some import duty relief."[1]

On February 23, 1716, the South Carolina Lords Proprietors, rulers of the colony, exempted from military duty Master Shipwright Benjamin Austin, eleven of his men, plus a sawyer, a caulker, and a joiner. They then exempted all goods arriving on South Carolina–built ships from import duties. Wragg and Danson's project was afoot.[2]

Charleston, like the rest of the British Empire,

simply would not have existed without seaborne transportation. Moving goods and people by sea throughout the empire was vital to its establishment, existence, and expansion. The empire was developed as a mercantile system to further the wealth and security of the English. Their relationships with the colonies were based on profitable trade, the emigration of undesirables, and military needs. Shipping provided the means to explore, conquer, and settle new territory in the seventeenth century. As the empire developed in the early eighteenth century, the British used ships to bring desired goods from the colonies to England for local consumption and re-exportation at a profit. In exchange, they usually sent out processed supplies and manufactured goods. Military vessels, and sometimes merchantmen, often were used to expand and protect the ports and sea lanes from foreign navies, privateers, and pirates.[3]

The transportation of goods, people, and information within the empire was conducted primarily on merchant vessels of various sizes and designs. Transatlantic merchantmen left the British Isles for America with settlers, soldiers, food supplies, and manufactured items. They usually returned nine months later with a few passengers and lightly processed cargoes such as mast stock, naval stores, tobacco, food, and indigo.

In order to buy necessary finished manufactures, such as tools and glass, from other parts of the British Empire or foreign lands, the colonists needed to ship American goods overseas, where their foodstuffs, tobacco, and forest products were in high demand. Without developed industries, the American colonists mostly raised and caught food, grew tobacco, and harvested forest products. They consumed the majority of food within their respective colonies and shipped some

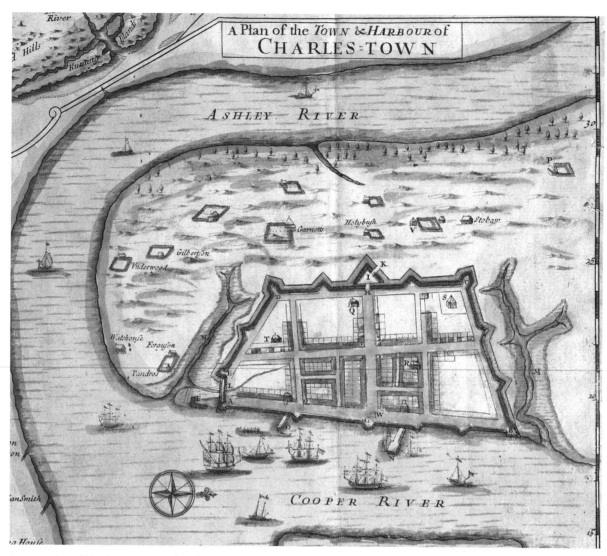

A c. 1717 plan of Charleston. *A compleat description of the province of Carolina in 3 parts* (London: Edward Crisp, c. 1717), *Collection of the Library of Congress, image g3870 ct001123.*

to other colonies and countries to obtain financial credit and other goods. Anglo-American colonists considered themselves British, citizens of the British Empire. They were British subjects, used British standards of measurements and money, and were protected by, and subject to, the British navigation and Admiralty laws.

Transatlantic voyages were often quite profitable when successful, but they were substantial endeavors for British American merchants in the eighteenth century. Raising the necessary capital to buy a ship and cargo, fitting out one's ship, hiring a good crew, and acquiring a cargo in America were only the first problems to address. Sailing to Britain or countries in southern Europe typically took two to three months of hard work. The Atlantic Ocean of the early and mid-eighteenth

century was not a friendly ocean for British merchantmen. Storms and disease were two natural problems that often worked against the crew, sometimes destroying the ship, crew, and cargo entirely. Pirates, privateers, and enemy cruisers were an almost constant hazard in the eighteenth century. When the ship neared its destination it was in danger of being wrecked on shore by weather or mistakes in piloting. Once in a European port the cargo was unloaded and sold, the ship was resupplied, and a westbound cargo was loaded. The port process commonly took one or two months. Then the ship sailed west through the same suite of hazards as before and with hard work and good fortune arrived in America to start the process again.

Consider the many variations to this tale. The

owner of the ship might invest in a cargo, a merchant might pay for the transportation of a few containers, or a merchant might hire an entire ship to carry a specific cargo for the voyage. Some ships were owned by companies that had monopolies in a particular trade. Some, such as the tobacco ships that sailed between England and Chesapeake Bay, often sailed in convoy, protected by a navy cruiser. When a profitable cargo was not available for a leg of a journey, captains would weight their ships with rocks or sand and sail "in ballast" to another port. Though most transatlantic ships sailed a shuttle route between two ports, some followed a multi-port pattern, and still others tramped from port to port as they saw an opportunity for greater profits or less danger. Generally, profit was the driving force that guided the ship owners, while costs and danger were their enemies.

During the first half of the eighteenth century, shipping and distribution costs within the British Empire steadily dropped in comparison to initial production costs of the goods transported. The drop in relative transportation costs was due mostly to an increase in port storage facilities, an increase in the size and weight of packaging, an increase in trade, and the destruction of most pirate enclaves. The development of port storage facilities, such as new quays and warehouses, and the increase of size and weight in packaging brought a great reduction of port time for ships and of inventory costs for the merchants. These factors, in turn, made it possible for some ships to make two roundtrips across the Atlantic per year instead of one. The increase in trade increased the flow of information about current markets around the Atlantic, and the destruction of pirate enclaves reduced losses and insurance rates.[4]

According to economic historians James Shepherd and Gary Walton, after these changes transportation and distribution costs were halved from 1675 to 1775, even while production costs increased by 14 percent. The new ratio of transportation to production costs promoted regional and social specialization in the empire. For example, in the American colonies English manufactured goods, such as tools, kitchenware, and clothing, often were better and cheaper, including the costs of transportation, than those produced in the colonies. Meanwhile colonists were able to deliver their products to English markets less expensively than before—tobacco, rice, timber products, deerskins, fish, and furs. As American overseas trade grew, it fostered an increase in America of settlements, domestic trade, employment, stock capital (mostly tools), dissemination of knowledge, immigration of trained people, and transfer of capital. All these forces, in turn, fostered maritime trade.[5]

The merchants of Charleston, South Carolina were active participants in these major changes of the Atlantic world. By Europe's standards, early eighteenth-century Charleston was a small town (only 3,500 people by 1720), yet it was the major port for the relatively new colony of South Carolina. Settled in 1670 by Englishmen who tried various cash crops, Charleston quickly developed a lucrative trade by shipping much of its rice crop and forest products, especially naval stores and deerskins, to London. Naval stores were supplies used for building and maintaining warships and merchantmen including lumber, masts, spars, heavy timbers, tar, pitch, and turpentine.

But Charleston, as the southernmost British city in North America, was in a precarious natural and geopolitical position. It was shaken by an earthquake and received much damage from a fire in 1698. In 1700 a destructive hurricane swept through. After a military force from Charleston unsuccessfully attacked Spanish St. Augustine, in 1706 a force of Spanish, French, and Indian raiders attacked the small city but was driven off. Hurricanes again pummeled Charleston in 1713 and 1714, but their effects on the colony were modest compared to the impact of the fierce Yamasee War (1715–17) with local tribes, in which many lives and much property were lost on both sides.

Natural disasters, local tribes, and European rivals were only some of the trials Charleston inhabitants faced. In the late 1600s pirates frequented the port as traders and customers for supplies and repairs. However, in the early 1700s, as the British began their eradication of piracy in the northern colonies and in the Bahamas, pirates shifted their operations to other areas and began to prey on the Charleston trade. Respecting the harbor fortifications the town had built for protection from French and Spanish ships, pirates could lie in wait just outside the harbor for merchantmen entering or leaving Charleston or ships sailing along the coast. In August 1717 the pirate Stede Bonnet, a retired British Army major, did just that, capturing two vessels within sight of shore while there was no navy ship to give chase.

Reading the letters and proclamations of the colonists one can see that through all these troubles, the people of South Carolina understood that their only means of communication with the outside world lay with the ships in Charleston Harbor. Yet the London merchants, owners of most of the large ships trading in the southern colonies, could realize better profits from the tobacco trade with Virginia and Maryland. Why should they place their ships in harm's way trading with Charleston? For the people of Charleston, having locally owned vessels that the Charleston merchants and authorities could use for their own purposes was imperative. So too was the development of shipbuilding and repair operations in their port. Timber and other naval stores were accessible, as was good shipbuilding terrain near navigable waters. Wragg and Danson's decision to commission the building of a large merchant ship in Charleston, to be named *Princess Carolina*, would have been considered essential to the colony's survival.[6]

As Stede Bonnet was capturing ships outside the harbor and the colonists were fighting the Yamasee in the forest, Master Shipwright Benjamin Austin was building and outfitting *Princess Carolina* in Charleston. He used a simple design that could be memorized and quickly drawn to build a 200-ton (London formula) ship that today we would consider a hybrid between a traditional British merchantman and a Dutch or French flyboat. Its flat bottom would help it carry a good load of cargo and yet sail over the sandbar that blocked Charleston's channel and into other shallow destinations. Austin was one of three owners of the new ship, but we do not know what his share of the ownership was or whether he bought his share with cash, credit, material, or his services as the shipwright.

Austin constructed *Princess Carolina*, unlike almost all other ships of her day, with wood from three different American colonies. Its major structural timbers were live oak, *Quercus virginiana*, but its planking was white oak, *Q. alba*. The live oak, growing nearby along the coast, would not have been a problem for them to harvest. However the Yamasee War made the forests too dangerous for harvesting the white oak planks. Austin later told Governor Johnson that although South Carolina white oak was superior to that from northern colonies, for the planks on the ship that he built for Wragg "the Indians Warr obliged them to send to Virginia and Rhode Island for plank."[7]

Austin built *Princess Carolina* four years after the war with France and Spain had ended and in the middle of Charleston's pirate troubles, so her four six-pounder gunports were not just for show. The crew and passengers might have to fight off pirates or foreign privateers at the mouth of their own harbor just to get to sea. When *Princess Carolina* first sailed from South Carolina in April 1718 the local clerk of the port recorded that Benjamin Austin was master (captain) and part owner. For the shipwright also to be a part owner and the master was uncommon but not unheard of. The other two listed owners of the ship were Jonathan Danson and William Wragg.[8]

Jonathan Danson was an important figure in early eighteenth-century Charleston. He married Mary Archdale, daughter of the governor, and through her in 1708 he inherited a position as one of the Lords Proprietors. Until 1719 South Carolina was a privately owned colony, and the Lords Proprietors were the appointed leaders of the colony. Evidently Danson had important personal business in England. Records show him taking the long roundtrip to London in 1699, 1711, and again in 1719.[9] William Wragg was a member of another prominent South Carolina family. His brother Samuel was named to the Great Council in 1717 and William was named to it in 1719.[10]

One could surmise that the owners named their ship with four things in mind: *Carolina*, the ship that first brought British settlers to Charleston in 1670; the name of their colony; a popular young noble, Princess Caroline, daughter-in-law of King George I; and her daughter Princess Caroline Elizabeth, who was called Carolina. Caroline—born Wilhelmine Karoline, princess of Brandenburg-Ansbach, in 1683—became a champion of the Protestant cause at the age of twenty by refusing to marry Archduke Charles, future Holy Roman Emperor, because she would have had to convert to Catholicism. Instead she married Prince George Augustus of Hanover, Germany, in 1705 and emigrated to England in 1714 when her father-in-law became George I of England. George Augustus and Caroline then became the prince and princess of Wales.

The British public generally was not fond of the Hanoverian royal family, especially since they preferred to speak their native German language, but Princess Caroline was the exception. Already popular as the princess who had refused a Catholic empire, she and her husband were more public and philanthropic when they arrived than the new king and queen from the Continent. She produced many children while surviving smallpox and pneumonia, holding the public's sympathetic attention. Her daughter Caroline was born in 1713. When her grandfather became George I she became a princess, but it seems that people probably called her "Princess Carolina" to distinguish her from her mother.[11] The name choice may also have been a reiteration of the owner's argument for the vessel's importance to the colony and reflected their thanks to the Lords Proprietors for making the ship possible. Using *Princess Carolina* for the ship's name might allow the owners to flatter both their home colony and the royal family without making it seem to their fellow colonists that they were honoring the "foreign" king. When dealing with the king's customs officers in London, which the owners planned to do, *Princess Carolina* might have been better than a name like *Friends' Adventure*.

South Carolina's leaders, only too aware of commerce's central place in the colony's survival and their personal well-being, were careful to support the colony's private enterprise sector, including overseas trade and shipbuilding. They had passed an act in 1703 that allowed a 50 percent discount on import and export duties for cargo in ships that were built and owned by South Carolinians. In 1716, the year before *Princess Carolina* was built, they passed an act that declared cargo on such ships to be duty free.[12] Import duties at the time included:

Dry goods
    10 percent
Slaves
    £10/head
Madeira wine
    £6/pipe (a cask of approximately 124 gallons)
Fayal wine
    £12/pipe

On a typical shipload of dry goods and Madeira wine, shippers using a South Carolina ship might save more than £1,000 in duties in Charleston. These savings alone would quickly pay for much of the cost of building a ship in South Carolina, giving it a distinct advantage over ships built elsewhere. Savvy businessmen, Austin, Danson, and Wragg probably had these duties in mind when they pooled their resources to build *Princess Carolina,* or they might have intended to build the ship and, with Danson being one of the Lords Proprietors, put pressure on the Great Council to enact the legislation. We can only speculate as none of their correspondence remains.

Princess Carolina's owners guaranteed that their ship would be given such status, even if the king's ministers overturned the laws, by registering the ship at Charleston in July 1717, nine months before she set sail.[13] Austin registered her in Charleston at 150 tons, meaning the ship could carry approximately 150 large wine casks called *tons* (approximately 240 gallons), the standard measurement unit for eighteenth-century merchant ships.

The owners also posted the necessary bond in the same month, much as certain businesses and people are required to be bonded today. To support the British mercantile system, which was to prove so profitable for most of the British colonies, merchant ship owners were required to post a bond to ensure their adherence to applicable laws. If a ship's master broke the British trade regulations by trading outside of the system without permission or trying to avoid government fees, the bond would be forfeited.

Most South Carolina food crops were grown for local consumption; however, early settlers also experimented with various crops and natural resources for overseas trade to pay for other goods that they wanted. By 1700 they had determined the export products that would set a pattern for Charleston trade during the early eighteenth century: rice, timber products, deer skins, and furs. On her maiden voyage from Charleston, *Princess Carolina's* cargo reflected Charleston's typical exports: rice, pitch, tar, turpentine, logwood, and hides (probably deerskins) for London.

Before they sailed, Benjamin Austin, as master, hired his crew. Later records indicate that *Princess Carolina* usually was manned by sixteen sailors and therefore was probably sailed by a similar number on her first voyage. At the time, sixteen was a common number of men for a transatlantic voyage on a ship of this size. The number of men was a balance reached by the owner between economy and perceived needs. All ships needed at least a minimum crew to work all the sails of the three masts in two watches (crews that stood four-hour watches together). More men were needed to man guns and repel hostile boarders in dangerous waters, to handle more sails in a fast ship, and to man the pumps in a leaky ship. Since *Princess Carolina* moved through the North Atlantic, an area rife with threats, she would have required more than a minimum crew of approximately twelve men.

A typical crew of sixteen men included the master, mate, boatswain, carpenter, gunner, cook, quartermaster, cooper, four able-bodied seamen, and four or five

THE ROYAL FAMILY OF GREAT BRITAIN

George II.d by the grace of God King of Great Brittain &c.

Caroline by the grace of God Queen of Great Brittain &c.

His Royal Highness Fredrick Prince of Wales Born January the 19.th 1706.

Her Highness Anne Princess Royal, Born October the 22.d 1709.

Her Highness Princess Amelia Sophia Elinora Born May the 30.th 1711.

Her Highness Princess Carolina Elizabeth Born May the 29.th 1713.

His Royal Highness William Duke of Cumberland &c. Born April the 15.th 1721.

Her Highness Princess Mary Born February the 22.d 1722.

Her Highness Princess Louisa Born December the 7.th 1724.

Princesses Caroline and Carolina with their family in the 1720s. *The Royal Family of Great Britain* (unknown artist, c.1725), Collection of National Portrait Gallery, London, image D3023.

ordinary seamen. The latter uncertainty exists because the naval officers did not record whether the "number of men" included the master. The master of a merchant vessel navigated and ruled the ship. He sometimes transacted business for the owners or consignees of the cargo. Sometimes the master was an owner or part owner of his ship and cargo. The mate, second in command, was responsible for one of the watches and management of the crew. The quartermaster helped the mate with administration and management of the crew. The boatswain guided the crew in maintaining the ship's rigging and hardware, while the carpenter maintained the hull, masts, and the ship's other wooden fixtures. The gunner tended the ordnance and munitions, while the cooper repaired or constructed any casks needed at sea and while in port. Able seamen were well experienced, while ordinary seamen still required more training. These were their duties in normal conditions, but on a good ship the crew helped one another with tasks, and during an emergency on any ship each of the crew did whatever was needed to save the ship.

Before loading a cargo, Austin also had to calculate the amount of ballast that would be needed to make *Princess Carolina* sail properly with a full load on the eastward journey. He had to consider many factors in his calculations, including the ship's draft, shape, and rigging, fair and foul weather to be expected, and the cargo's weight and density. South Carolina rice was shipped clean, without husk, and therefore was particularly dense, as were tar and pitch. Therefore the ship probably needed little, if any, ballast with its first cargo.[14] After the crew loaded any sand ballast needed into the hold they could begin to load their eastbound cargo through the main and forward cargo hatches.

The main and forward cargo hatches on the ship were rectangular, 4 feet by 6 feet for the main hatch and 4 feet by 5 feet for the forward hatch, with their long dimension running fore-and-aft. This meant that the barrels of rice and naval stores could easily be lowered into the hold horizontally and longitudinally, and most likely they were stored that way. This technique of stowing seems to have been standard in the Western world. Early evidence includes the remains of the 1565 Basque whaling ship excavated at Red Bay, Labrador.[15] Schooner captains still used the same stowing method, *bilge and cantline* (or *cutline*), through the early twentieth century.

Most of Austin's cargo was naval stores, including 748 barrels of tar (collected from the ends of pine logs when heated), 536 barrels of pitch (a refined tar),

and 181 barrels of turpentine (distilled from pine sap). Turpentine was used in preservatives and as a disinfectant and was the common solvent for tar, pitch, and paints. In England tar and pitch, usually obtained from Sweden, were supplies valued for the expanding British navy and merchant fleet. They were the major preservatives for the wood and hemp lines that made up the ships' hulls and rigging. Since the Swedes had restricted some of the exportation of naval stores to being carried only on Swedish merchant vessels, Parliament began paying a bounty for American tar and pitch in 1704.[16]

Shipping naval stores presented the captain with certain headaches, literally and figuratively. All three liquids produced fumes that would ruin food cargo such as rice if they were stored near such cargo. Turpentine fumes were also known to affect the crew's minds and physical health. To reduce the problems, Austin likely would have stored only the barrels of naval stores in the main cargo hold, below the lower deck. Each layer of casks above the first was staggered both fore-and-aft and athwart ships so that the bilge (widest section) of each cask fitted into a hollow formed by the casks' ends in the lower layer. They were chocked with broken cask staves, triangular chocks, or dunnage (usually small tree limbs) such as we observed during archaeological excavations of other ship sites. Interstices at either end of the hold, formed by the shifted tiers of casks, were generally filled with more dunnage, since the fumes would preclude most other cargo being in the same hold.[17]

Naval stores also could cause nightmarish disasters at sea. Barrels of tar were prone to leak, and possibly burst, in warm weather as tar expanded when warm. Tar or pitch oozing into the bilge, and thence into the pump well, would quickly clog the bilge pumps. In the middle of the North Atlantic, a month away from land in either direction and with no means of calling for assistance, clogged bilge pumps on a wooden ship were a serious emergency. A leak or storm without working pumps could cause the loss of the ship and crew without a trace. As the standard eighteenth-century solvent for tar, some turpentine was always stowed for easy access when carrying naval stores in case of needing to clear the bilge pumps. Care also had to be taken when working in the hold. Any open flame from a lamp or match could ignite a fire or explosion with such a flammable cargo.[18]

A more benign cargo, rice was a major export crop

THE LOGWOOD BUSINESS was more complex than it might appear. The tree, *Haematoxylum campechianum*, growing in the swamps of Central America's coast, had a particularly hard, dense wood. The British cloth industry was after its heartwood, which when chipped and immersed in water produced a red dye. The color of the dye could be changed to different shades of purple and blue, or used as a base for other colors, by shifting the solution's pH balance. The price of logwood varied widely since both demand and supplies of the commodity often changed due to many uncontrolled variables.

In the seventeenth and early eighteenth centuries individuals and firms, mostly from British America, struggled in the business along the Yucatan Peninsula coast. Harvesting and delivering logwood was a difficult and dangerous endeavor, sometimes bringing great wealth and sometimes bringing financial ruin or death. In the insect-infested tropical swamps, cutting crews consisted of individuals, hired workers, indentured servants, and slaves. They waded through and stood in murky waters for hours each day, using saws and axes to drop the hard, gnarly trees. They were after the trunk's heartwood, so they limbed the tree and cut off its outer bark and sapwood, leaving tangles of discarded wood behind. Crews then had to carry the wood, which was too dense to float, to a storing area along the coast. On the coast, logwood was loaded onto small coasting vessels for delivery to intermediary ports such as New York, Charleston, and Jamaica for transshipment to the Old World, or was loaded into large ships for a direct transatlantic voyage. When logwood was mixed with other cargos one needed to be careful to separate it from things that owners might not want dyed red.

Life was hard and dangerous on the Yucatan coast. The men and a few women lived in various conditions, but usually on their vessels or in huts built on stilts above the water. During the day and night swarms of disease-carrying mosquitoes and other biting insects attacked them. While they worked the cutters were prey to snakes, leaches, various parasitic worms, and alligators. They were injured and killed by accidents made more frequent by the swamps' dangerous footing and the extensive use of alcohol. Slaves, workers, and bosses were killed by their owners, their equals, or rebelling slaves.

Dangers also came from outside the swamps. Hurricanes and smaller storms could kill people on land and sea. Pirates also attacked on land and sea. Spain tried to enforce its claim to the territory and its wood by sending naval vessels and issuing privateering licenses for ships to capture the British logwood vessels and crews as they left with their valuable cargos. Taking the vessel and logwood, the Spanish often marooned the British sailors to die slowly on a desert island or imprisoned them to die slowly in overcrowded tropical prison ships. The Spanish occasionally attacked the cutting crews and the cargo vessels by land. It was a large land attack that forced the logwood cutters out of the Bay of Campeche, south to new camps on the Bay of Honduras in 1716, in an area that is now in the country of Belize. The loss of capital and disruption in supply as they reestablished themselves on the southwestern coast of the Yucatan probably greatly elevated the volatile price of logwood in Europe. Therefore in 1718 *Princess Carolina's* ten tons of logwood might have brought a very good price in London.*

* Geoffrey L. Rossano, "Who's Afraid to Go to the Bay? Colonial Shippers and the Central American Logwood Trade 1670–1770," in *Global Crossroads and the American Seas* (Missoula, Montana: Pictoral Histories, 1988), 19–25; Rossano, "Down to the Bay: New York Shippers and the Central American Logwood Trade, 1748–1761," *New York History Quarterly* 70, no. 3 (1989): 228–50; Carl and Roberta Bridenbaugh, *No Peace Beyond the Line: The English in the Caribbean 1624–1690* (New York: Oxford University Press, 1972), 338–42.

of South Carolina. British Carolinians, not knowing much about rice farming, purposely imported slaves from the rice growing regions of Africa to start and augment their expanding plantations.[19] The listed 263 barrels of rice would have been loaded after the naval stores, probably between the lower and upper decks. This would keep the rice relatively free of naval store fumes and protected from the weather and seas. Since rice had to be kept dry on the voyage, barrels of rice on the bottom layer were generally stowed *bilge free*; that is, they rested on dunnage to keep their sides well

off the deck in case the deck became wet. More dunnage would keep the barrels from touching the ceiling planking on the side of the ship.[20]

Rice cargo did present certain challenges to the crew during the voyage. Since rice generally was still slow-drying when loaded, the moisture released through the barrel staves had to be vented from the storage area to prevent rotting of the ship and the collection of moisture on the underside of the deck above. Dripping condensate could ruin the upper tiers of rice. In addition, care was needed to keep the cargo area as dry as possible at all times. Excess water on the deck would not only ruin the cargo but might also swell the rice, causing the lower tier of barrels to burst and collapse, shifting the cargo, and causing a dangerous situation in high seas. The ten chests of skins were probably stowed forward and aft of the rice, tucked into spaces left by the staggered rows of rice barrels and lending stability to the casks.

The 10 tons of logwood were likely stowed on the weather deck in the waist, or middle, of the ship. In the eighteenth-century Atlantic world, *logwood* was a particular species of wood, mostly gathered in Central America, which when processed provided a number of dyes important to Britain's and Europe's growing cloth industries. The logs would be easily loaded and unloaded free of the hatches at any time and would not be ruined by fresh or salt water on the voyage. If the crew found themselves in a dangerous situation at sea, they could unfasten the wood and toss it over the side.

Princess Carolina's hull shape, the height of the decks, and the position of the hatches provide information about the distribution of cargo in the hold. Knowing the space required for the cargo allows the determination of space remaining for other uses and of weight distribution in the vessel. These in turn allow the determination of the amount of ballast required for the ship to be stable and of some sailing characteristics of the ship.

Four small cannon would have been kept ready in the ship's after section between decks, two on each side. In addition, the captain, mate, quartermaster, and important passengers traditionally quartered at that level in the stern. The crew and common passengers' berthing areas were determined by the stowage of the cargo, which had to be kept safe and stowed correctly to help the ship sail properly. The only remaining areas for their quarters were in the forecastle and among the ordnance. Space had to be left around the cannon so that they might be used against an attack, so this might have been the best common berthing area. The small forecastle was another possible area, but traditionally it was the gathering and feeding compartment for the crew.

Once the cargo was in place the master would check the trim (level) of his vessel, usually by being rowed around it in still waters. A comparison of bow and stern draft marks—numbers marking every foot up from the keel's bottom—helped the master determine the ship's fore-and-aft trim. After the crew made any

necessary changes in trim by shifting the cargo and ballast, the ship would be ready for its transatlantic voyage. At that time Austin would have reported his imminent sailing to the local naval officer, or clerk of the Naval Office, who represented the governor in local shipping matters. The clerk inspected the ship's papers, granted a certificate of clearance, and recorded information about the ship, crew, and cargo in the Naval Office Shipping Lists. The following information was recorded for the merchantman *Princess Carolina* by the Charleston naval officer on April 3, 1718:[21]

Cleared from Charlestown

Time of clearing – April 3, 1718	Ship's name – *Princess Carolina*
Of what place [registered port] – Carolina	Master's name – Austin, Benj.
Kind of build – Square [sterned] ship	Tons (registered) – 150
When & where built – Carolina, 1717	
When & where registered – Carolina, July 1717	
Owners – Benj. Austin, Jno. Danson, Wm. Wragg	
Whither bound – London	
When & where bond given – Carolina, July 8, 1717	

Cargo Exported:

263 barrels of rice	536 barrels of pitch
748 barrels of tar	181 barrels of turpentine
10 tons of logwood	10 chests of skins

After providing information to the naval officer, Austin could sail from Charleston for London when the wind and weather were right and there were no pirates in sight.

Though the Charleston port records indicate that *Princess Carolina* sailed from Charleston for London on April 3, 1718, no London port records exist from 1718 to 1725, as they were purposely destroyed to make room for "more important" records in the late nineteenth century. Thus we do not know when Austin arrived in England. Two months would have been a typical passage from Charleston to London in the spring. Austin probably took advantage of the currents and trade winds that would have taken the ship north-northeast, past New York, New England, and Newfoundland and then east to the British Isles. Spring and summer are the best times for sailing in the North Atlantic, so they may have had fairly good weather, though violent storms could strike at any time.

Crossing the Atlantic on a fully loaded merchant ship in 1718 would not be a comfortable journey for

TWO MONTHS AFTER Austin cleared the harbor for London, a letter was written from Charleston describing an event on May 22, 1718:

"Sir, . . . Cpt. Mede . . . proceeding from the bar [sand bar at the harbor entrance] was unfortunately taken by two pirates, one a large French ship mounted with 40 guns and the other a sloop mounted with 12 guns with two other sloops for their tenders, having in all about 300 men all English the ship is commanded by one Theach"*

Blackbeard, the notorious pirate, had arrived in his forty-gun *Queen Anne's Revenge* to blockade Charleston Harbor. He had with him two smaller ships, including that of Stede Bonnet, who had probably suggested the adventure after his success off Charleston the year before. On one of the ships that the pirates captured were William Wragg's brother Samuel and Samuel's four-year-old son William, who had intended to sail from Charleston for London, only to be captured at the mouth of the harbor by Blackbeard. The pirates held them for several days, threatening their lives a number of times, until they were ransomed. The younger William later became a famous chief justice and member of the Great Council of South Carolina.**

* Unsigned letter to Sirs, June 13, 1718, *Records in the BPRO South Carolina*, 7: 74.
** *Records in the BPRO South Carolina*, 7: 74–93; Letter from Gov. Johnson to Your Lordships, June 18, 1718, *Records in the BPRO South Carolina*, 7: 134–36.

anyone. The captain and crew had to sail and maintain the ship on a twenty-four-hour schedule. Food rations for such a voyage were sometimes better, sometimes worse than on shore, but crew and common passengers slept where they could find room. In good weather they might sleep on the weather deck while the hatches were cracked open to air the cargo. However, when the weather was bad, living space was minimal. For sleeping, they could find shelter from the weather and storm waves only between the decks, aft of the rice and skins cargo and forward of the officers' quarters. With the hatches closed they would have had to share this space with four cannon and fumes from the rice cargo, which produced a repulsive smell when drying in a closed space. The crew would spend approximately two months of working, eating, and resting in such conditions to reach London.

On the Thames River, Austin and the crew would have found a vibrant port from the mouth of the river to London. The Romans had started using cribbing and fill to create wharves along the Thames, and by the eighteenth century, to accommodate oceanic shipping, Londoners had built wharves that extended for miles along the river's south shore. As in any busy port, the crew from provincial Charleston needed to be wary to protect themselves, ship, and cargo from vermin and thieves. By 1718 Britain's empire was expanding rapidly around the world, and London, with a population near 600,000 people, was the political, economic, and social center of the empire. *Princess Carolina's* crew would have marveled at the sights and smells of the bustling new fish market nearby at Billingsgate, the recently built Buckingham Palace and St. Paul's Cathedral, and city streets that had been lit by oil lamps for decades.

The crew may have been anxious about the political climate in London. Before they left Charleston there had been news of the serious rift between King George I and his son, the husband of their ship's namesake. Prince George had been banished from the royal household the previous summer but forced to leave his children with the king. Caroline left with her husband but was allowed daily visits with her children.

The port area of London processed not only cargoes moving to and from its surrounding area but also foreign goods bound for the colonies. All goods imported from other countries and bound for the colonies, except for salt and wine from the Iberian peninsula and islands, first had to be inspected and taxed in the area called Legal Quays of London. For example, tea, spices, and other Asian goods destined for South Carolina were generally brought from their source by the East India Company ships to London, where they were unloaded and inspected, customs were paid, and the goods were loaded on ships bound for Charleston.

In London the Charleston merchants, represented by Austin, a London agent, or their own factor in London, would receive credit or notes for their cargo on *Princess Carolina*. In addition they would apply to the authorities for naval stores bounty. One can estimate their gross income for the voyage by using some price figures that pertained generally from 1715 to 1720, though we must realize that prices were in constant flux and varied from port to port, depending upon the shippers, ownership situations, and sales agreements. For these figures let us assume that all the cargo arrived in good condition.

Bounties from British government:[22]

748 barrels of tar @ £4 per 8 barrels	£374
536 barrels of pitch @ £4 per 8 barrels	268
181 barrels of turpentine @ £3 per 8 barrels	68
Total	£710

Income from sales:[23]

748 barrels of tar @ 14s (£0.7) per barrel	524
536 barrels of pitch @ 21s (£1.05) per barrel	563
181 barrels of turpentine @ 15s per barrel[1]	136
263 barrels of rice @ 25s (£1.25) per barrel	329
10 tons of logwood @ £2.8 per ton[2]	28
10 chests of skins @ unknown	?
Estimated subtotal from sales	£1,580
Estimated subtotal from bounties	£710
Estimated total from cargo, less the skins	£2,290

1. Franklin Coyne, *The Development of the Cooperage Industry in the United States, 1620–1940* (Chicago: Lumer Buyers Publishing, 1940), 13; William Beveridge, *Prices and Wages in England from the Twelfth to the Nineteenth Century* (London: Frank Cass and Company, 1965) 660–66, 741.
2. Bart Kahr, S. Lovell, and J. A. Subramony, "The Progress of Logwood Extract," *Chirality* 10 (1998): 70.

With their credit the merchants could buy, often via the same representative who sold their cargo, all manner of British and foreign goods to sell in Charleston. The colonists needed a wide variety of goods, mostly British, to survive in America. With the return cargo purchased, Austin would again calculate the needed amount and placing of ballast, would load and trim the ship, and would register with officials to depart the Thames. He then would take advantage of the wind and tide to start his return journey. In January 1719 Austin returned to Charleston with the ship carrying "Sundry Goods as pr: Cocketts."[24] This meant that when he arrived in Charleston the various British and foreign goods, for which any appropriate customs had been paid, were listed on a London-issued customs officer's form, called a cocket (sometimes spelled cockett or coquett).

Three months after arriving in Charleston, Austin sailed *Princess Carolina* to London again, with 416 barrels of rice, 626 barrels of pitch, 811 barrels of tar, and 2 chests and a bag of deer skins.[25] Arriving in London, or possibly before that, he seems to have relinquished his share in the ship to Micajah (also Mica) Perry, who registered her in London on December 4, 1719.

Interestingly, Perry registered *Princess Carolina* as 150 tons in London, though before and after that the same ship was always recorded as 150 tons in America and 200 tons in London.[26]

Micajah was the grandson of Micaiah Perry, the most prominent trader, commission agent, shipper, and financier of American colonial trade, especially to Charleston, Virginia, Philadelphia, and New York. The London-based Perry and Company bought and sold goods, did the same on commission for many of the wealthier colonial merchants and plantation owners of the Chesapeake and Carolinas, shipped the goods in space they rented on ships, and extended to the colonists great sums of credit when needed to keep the cargos moving across the Atlantic through economic expansion and recession. Micajah was part of the firm and was actually baptized Macaiah, but signed his name with a "long i" to distinguish himself from his grandfather. Rather than rent space on ships, as was his grandfather's standard practice, Macajah preferred to be a part owner, and sometimes majority owner, of a number of merchant ships so that he could send them where he needed them most. When the elder Micaiah died in 1721, twenty-six-year-old Micajah became the firm's senior partner.[27]

At least for its first two years *Princess Carolina* had been involved with a shuttle trade between London and Charleston, carrying wanted goods directly to each entrepôt. Without having to pay import and export duties at the Charleston end and receiving £710 in bounties for naval stores in London, the ship's owners were probably enjoying a quality business experience. However, economic woes were about to strike Great Britain as the great South Seas bubble burst in 1720, sending the Atlantic Rim economies into a recession; they were saved from complete destruction only by European governments stabilizing the banks.

Because the British merchant shipping records from the next few years were destroyed long ago, we do not know what happened to *Princess Carolina* during the recession and can only pick up the story almost five years later. Perry's new share of the ship seems to have influenced its voyages as *Princess Carolina* was traveling to different ports, carrying various cargos.

In September 1724 a new master, William Halladay (also Holiday, Holliday, and Hollyday), sailed *Princess Carolina* into London, but we do not know from where. There is no mention of the cargo or any passengers, but there is a count of sixteen crewmen.[28] One might

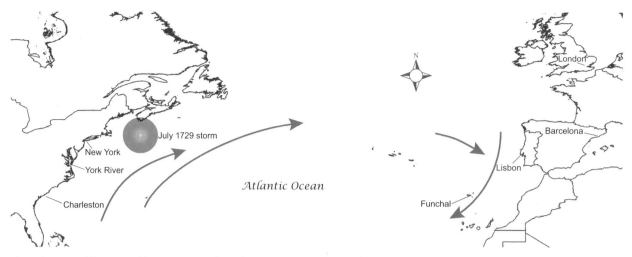

The Atlantic world navigated by *Princess Carolina*, showing its known ports of call and trade winds. *Illustration by Warren Riess.*

question if, after five years, this was the same ship, but subsequent records include that Halladay's *Princess Carolina* was built in 1717 in Charleston, was the same size, had the same number of crew and guns as Austin's ship, and was owned by the same men, except that Perry replaced Austin as one of the owners.

On April 1, 1725, Halladay brought the ship into the East River alongside New York City "in ballast" from London. In ballast meant her holds were empty, except for extra ballast to allow proper sailing without the weight of a cargo. The owners listed in 1725 were Halladay, Perry, Danson, and Wragg.[29] Benjamin Austin, by 1724 no longer associated with *Princess Carolina*, remained in Charleston and became master and possibly sole owner of the merchant sloop *Orange*.[30]

New York was one of the largest ports in America at the time, though with only some seven thousand inhabitants, the city was smaller than Charleston. *Princess Carolina's* masts, standing perhaps eighty feet high, would have towered over the town's buildings. Yet the port had been established a century earlier by the Dutch for overseas trade and was easily able to provide Halladay with the cargo and stores he needed. The population and commerce of the colony of New York were growing rapidly in the 1720s. Settlers were moving into the newly opened hinterlands up the Hudson River. They needed goods from afar and produced export crops, mostly grains. They also sold forest products, especially lumber and cask staves, as they cleared the land for farming.

On Manhattan the inhabitants continued to improve and expand their waterfront, constructing wharves and building quays along the shore. They built new residential and commercial buildings, including warehouses, as their economy and population grew. Unloading excess ballast from *Princess Carolina* and loading the ship with cargo and supplies, even from a nearby warehouse, would take many days of labor; the boatswain and carpenter would meanwhile be overseeing any needed repairs. After a four-week stay, the ship sailed on April 29 for Lisbon, Portugal, with a cargo of grain and lumber.[31]

Portugal was a small country that possessed an extensive empire and trading network around the world. Though they enjoyed limited natural resources in their homeland, the Portuguese were able to export ocean and orchard products such as olive oil and fish. From Africa, Asia, and the Americas they imported what they needed and traded with the rest of Europe and the British Isles. At Lisbon, as Halladay and his crew sailed into the Tagus River, they would have sailed by the old Torre de Belém, a handsome fortress standing out from the shore, and would then have found themselves at an ancient trading port within a well-protected harbor. Ships from around the world were loaded and unloaded either while moored, using small boats, or by hand while secured parallel to the quays that extended along a portion of the shore. Even more than in London, the crew would know they were in a cosmopolitan port where people spoke many languages, used various monetary and measuring systems, and practiced exotic customs. Here Halladay could sell or deliver his grain and lumber to be used in Portugal or be traded to others in Europe. Here also, in the middle of shipworm spawning season, *Princess Carolina* would have been surrounded by ships infested with shipworms from many oceans. Lisbon and some of the other Iberian ports at which she was to moor in the summer months were probably where the shipworms that were to help identify the ship centuries later entered the ship's wood.

Upon leaving Lisbon it appears that Halladay sailed to Barcelona, Spain, for an unknown reason.[32] Perhaps he heard he could get a better price for all or part of his cargo there, or that Micajah Perry had arranged for his grain or lumber to be taken to Barcelona. Barcelona, on the Mediterranean side of the Iberian Peninsula, was a large and ancient city that would serve ships and cargos not only from the Mediterranean but also from many regions in the Atlantic and Pacific oceans and the Caribbean. Already in the thirteenth century Barcelona's population had outgrown the surrounding region's food surpluses, forcing the city to import food, especially grains. However, the city had no natural harbor, requiring deep-keeled ships to be moored offshore while they were tended by lighters working from the beach. Between the beach and the city was a high stone wall, protected by intersecting lines of fire from fortress and battery cannon.[33] Halladay would have been able to bring *Princess Carolina*, with her twelve-foot draft, closer to the city than most large ocean-crossing ships could go. There he would unload his cargo and pick up provisions and perhaps goods for a return voyage.

On March 17, 1726, a year after leaving New York, *Princess Carolina* sailed into the Chesapeake Bay from Barcelona.[34] Whereas the naval officer in Yorktown, Virginia, was careful to record every entering and departing ship's cargo, he listed nothing in *Princess Carolina* when it arrived. Halladay may again have been sailing in ballast, but it is hard to imagine him leaving Barcelona without some of the desired Catalan brandy or almond oil.[35] We do not know if he came in empty-handed or simply paid off the clerk with coin or goods from Lisbon or Barcelona. If he had no cargo to transport from the Iberians, he may have had orders from Perry to sail from Barcelona as soon as possible to Virginia to carry a shipment of tobacco out of the Chesapeake while it was freshly packed and before shipworm spawning season.

The Chesapeake is an extensive complex of bay, rivers, streams, and intertidal flats; its limited depth made it a natural trading terminus for the shallow-draft *Princess Carolina*. In the early eighteenth century the region annually produced thousands of tons of tobacco for export to the British Isles, where it was used and also sold to the continental countries. In return, the people of the Chesapeake required all manner of manufactured goods, food, and supplies for themselves and to sell to other colonies. Chesapeake planters relied on others for shipping as it was economically

better for the colonists to spend their and their slaves' labor clearing the forest, raising tobacco, and using the profits to buy what they needed.[36]

Micajah Perry had extensive trading connections in Virginia, where the Perry firm had been financing and trading for a 2.5 percent commission with the wealthier plantation owners of the York, James, and Rappahannock rivers for decades—shipping the planters' high grade tobacco to London, selling it there, then purchasing and shipping to the Chesapeake the requested return cargos. Three of Perry and Company's substantial clients, or "correspondents," were the well-known Virginians John Custis, Robert Carter, and William Byrd II, while William Randolph had been a client until his death in 1711. Historian Jacob Price estimated that in the year 1719 Perry and Company grossed £4,600 from Virginia commissions alone.[37] Two months after arriving, *Princes Carolina* cleared out of Yorktown, Virginia, on June 24, 1726, for London, with 554 hogsheads of tobacco and 2,920 pipe staves (described later).[38]

In the early eighteenth century most merchant ships of more than 100 tons visiting the Chesapeake left with tobacco for London. Tobacco was a fragile commodity, prone to damage when handled or transported by wagon along America's poor roads.[39] Since inter-Chesapeake transportation of tobacco was expensive and dangerous for the cargo, and shallow-draft ships could navigate up most rivers in the Chesapeake, few entrepôt cities developed in the Chesapeake until later. Instead, the ships typically anchored near large plantations to buy tobacco or ship it on consignment for a local planter or a London merchant.[40] The Chesapeake purchases typically were transacted by factors for the English tobacco merchants before the ship was ready to load. However, the wealthier plantation owners often preferred to ship their tobacco to London for a better profit, mostly using the Perry firm as agent to do so. Since Perry was principal owner of *Princess Carolina*, Halladay was probably shipping tobacco for Custis, Carter, or Byrd.

At the plantations, crews typically could not bring the ship over the very shallow oyster flats that extended a quarter mile out from the shore. Small boats belonging to the ship and the plantation owner were used to row casks of tobacco to the ship's side. There each cask was hoisted up and into the ship's hold using the mainmast, a spar as a boom crane, and a capstan or windlass. In contemporary illustrations and present rigging practice, casks on their sides were lifted using a double loop sling or barrel hitch.

ON ITS FOUR VISITS to Virginia (1726–29), *Princess Carolina,* as one of Perry's best ships for maneuvering in Chesapeake Bay, probably carried goods one or more times for three of Virginia's most prominent planters. I have not found records of who owned its cargo on any of the voyages. However, Micajah Perry tried to represent only planters and merchants who could supply high quality goods in sufficient quantity to fill the holds of his ships, and he sent *Princess Carolina* directly into the rivers that bordered the lands of three of his best clients: John Custis, Robert Carter, and William Byrd II.*

John Custis (1678–1749) was well known to the Perry firm, because as a young Virginia gentleman he had studied the merchant trade in London with the Perry firm, under the tutelage of Micajah's grandfather. With his own father's and grandfather's guidance and support, and the knowledge he acquired from the elder Perry, Custis became one of the most successful tobacco planters in the American colonies. He owned thousands of acres, worked by more than a hundred slaves, and was active in Virginia politics. Through marriage he was related to William Byrd II and was considered one of "the better sort" who were the social, economic, and political leaders of Virginia. Custis lived on Francis Street in Williamsburg, where he established a renowned garden of almost four acres and a notable fine arts collection.**

Robert Carter (c. 1664–1732) was the richest man in Virginia, sometimes referred to as "King Carter." He inherited much and acquired more, owning more than a quarter million acres of Virginia land when he died. Like Custis, Carter learned the Atlantic merchant trade from his Virginia family and years at the home of a London merchant. He lived at Corotoman, about twenty-five miles north of Williamsburg, where in 1725 he built the largest home in Virginia. While most of his tilled land furnished food for his family, slaves, and employees, Carter acquired wealth through the shrewd growing and selling of tobacco and food, rents of land and small water vessels, and activity in slave trading. He was quite successful in politics, eventually becoming senior member of the Governor's Council.***

William Byrd II (1674–1744) was born in Virginia but spent most of his first thirty years studying business, languages, and law and practicing law in London. When his father died he returned to Virginia, inheriting great wealth. His plantation, like the others, produced much food and tobacco. Through the decades Byrd's economic and political life surged and waned. He crossed the Atlantic a number of times on personal and colonial business, and each time he lived in Virginia he improved the family estate of Westover Plantation, approximately eighteen miles west of Williamsburg. There he accumulated one of the best libraries in America and wrote some notable books and essays. Byrd and John Custis married sisters, thus loosely uniting two of the most powerful families in Virginia.†

While Micajah Perry's firm represented all three of these powerful Virginians in London transactions, he was not the only London agent that they used. The colonists were careful to spread their business around so that they might attain the best prices when selling or buying, and one can see from Custis's surviving letters that he used the threat of shifting to another agent whenever he was unhappy with Perry.†† Yet their letters seem to imply hardnosed business practices among friends. In 1728 Byrd wrote to Perry that some Virginians, rather than investing in tobacco when there was a glut on the market, were investing in mining ventures in western Virginia, and he seemed to be warning Perry that it was an economic bubble "as the south sea phrenzy." †††

* These three men are repeatedly mentioned in Jacob Price's *Perry of London* (Cambridge, Mass.: Harvard University Press, 1992).

** Sara Bearss, "John Custis (1678–1749)," in *Dictionary of Virginia Biography*, vol. 3, ed. John Kneebone (Richmond: Library of Virginia, 2006).

*** Edmund Berkeley, "Robert Carter (1664–1732)," in *Dictionary of Virginia Biography*, vol. 3, ed. John Kneebone (Richmond: Library of Virginia, 2006).

† Pierre Marambaud, *William Byrd of Westover, 1674–1744* (Charlottesville: University Press of Virginia, 1971).

†† John Custis, *The Letterbook of John Custis IV of Williamsburg 1717–1742*, ed. Josephine Little Zuppen (New York: Rowman and Littlefield, 2005), 91.

††† Marion Tinling (ed.), *The Correspondence of the Three William Byrds of Westover, Virginia 1684–1776* (Charlottesville: University Press of Virginia), vol. 1, 377–78.

Tobacco generally was shipped in hogsheads (pronounced "hogs'hids" in Virginia today), which were wooden casks made of staves, two heads, and wooden hoops. They varied in size, depending on their contents, origin, and date. Tobacco hogsheads in 1726 Virginia had been standardized in 1695 at inside dimensions of 46 inches high by 30 inches diameter at the heads, or outside dimensions of 48 inches high by 35 inches diameter at the bilge (bulge in the middle). Their capacity was approximately 63 gallons. Tobacco, like most commodities in the eighteenth century, was sold by the pound, but because it was light for its volume, a ship's capacity for tobacco was limited by space, not weight. This required a ship's owner(s) to charge by volume rather than by weight. Since tobacco's value was by weight, and transportation costs were by volume, shippers gradually learned to pack more tobacco into the hogsheads by using a pressing technique that did not harm the tobacco. Thus a Virginia hogshead contained approximately 600 pounds of tobacco in the seventeenth century and 650 pounds of tobacco in 1724.[41]

The 2,920 pipe staves leaving in the ship were components for large casks. A pipe was a cask holding approximately 120 gallons (this also varied by place and year), about twice the capacity of a hogshead and half the capacity of a ton/tun. Chesapeake farmers and their slaves produced thousands of barrel, hogshead, and pipe staves each year for their own use and to sell as they cleared land for tobacco and food production.

Tobacco, especially the high quality leaf that Perry's clients produced, was an expensive cargo that was not as sensitive to moisture as was rice, but once wet it was worthless. The sailors and officers would have made sure to secure the tobacco hogsheads in *Princess Carolina's* main cargo hold, between decks, and in any other dry areas. Pipe staves would have been placed under, above, and around the precious tobacco hogsheads to keep them away from any moisture and to keep them from moving in a storm. Though masters sometimes carried extra tobacco on the open weather deck covered by tarpaulins, they assumed it would bring a low price, if any, in England.

Princess Carolina arrived in London on September 2, seventy-one days after clearing the Chesapeake.[42] Halladay must have made efficient use of his time in port as he returned to Yorktown, Virginia, on February 18, 1727, from London and Funchal, Madeira, with 31 pipes of wine and "Sundry European goods per Cocqt."[43] One might speculate that Halladay had unloaded his tobacco in London, loaded an unknown amount of various European goods, sailed to Madeira to deliver the pipe staves and load a cargo of wine, then sailed for Virginia.

Madeira port records from between 1718 and the second half of 1727 have not survived, but it is reasonable to hypothesize that Captains Austin and Halladay may have made visits to Madeira on previous westbound voyages as its geography, weather, and location in the Atlantic Ocean made it an island perfect for providing fresh, clean water and producing food and wine. If a captain bought "supplies for the voyage" in Madeira, they would not have been recorded by a government clerk when the ship entered an American port. Most wine imbibed by British colonists in the first half of the eighteenth century came from Portuguese Madeira, to which many British winemakers and merchants had moved in the late seventeenth century. Their business connections with London and all the British colonies were extensive.

Funchal, the capital and largest port in Madeira, serviced ocean-sailing ships that came for its wine and for supplies and repairs as they crossed the Atlantic on their voyages to and from Europe, North and South America, Africa, and the Far East. While the Madeira winemakers and merchants were good at providing the right wine varieties and amount of fortification for their customers, and each American colony seemed to have its own preferred Madeira wine, it was not until the last half of the eighteenth century that much of the Madeira wine was fortified with brandy. The wine Halladay carried into Virginia for the Chesapeake planters was closer to a continental red wine than to modern fortified Madeira.[44]

A portion of the goods on board may well have been the latest glassware for presenting and drinking wine. Wealthier Virginia planters and merchants enjoyed using the latest English customs, including transporting wine from a storage cask to the table in a decanter made of leaded crystal. The early eighteenth century witnessed a simplification in tableware design, including decanters that were commonly six- or eight-sided, with a long neck. Crystal wine glasses also had become less ornate, so that their stems, though varied, were most likely to be formed with a series of shapes, each round in cross section.

On June 24, 1727, exactly a year after his previous voyage started, Halladay again sailed *Princess Carolina* out of the York River to transport 547 hogsheads of tobacco and 3,000 pipe staves, arriving in London on September 3, 1726. After offloading, cleaning, and victualing, Halladay left London, apparently with no cargo destined for the American colonies, to arrive in Funchal, Madeira, on November 11, 1727. Three days later *Princess Carolina* set sail for Virginia.[45] The weather must have been favorable, as the port clerk recorded the ship arriving in Yorktown sixteen days after it left Funchal, with 46 pipes and 12 hogsheads of wine.[46]

Halladay then repeated the triangular trading trip in 1728, arriving at London in September, reaching Madeira in October, and returning to the York River in November with 71 pipes and 2 hogsheads of wine.[47] Note that in these voyages *Princess Carolina's* cargo hold was not full. The important leg of the roundtrip was eastbound, carrying as much tobacco as possible from Virginia to London.

While in Virginia Halladay again loaded tobacco and then gathered in the spring and early summer of 1729 with many other merchantmen to await a Royal Navy escort because Spanish privateers were off the coast of Virginia, trying to capture merchant ships. Earlier, Captain Joseph Lingen, commander of the forty-gun royal warship *Ludlow Castle* had left the Downs (off southeast England) on October 15, 1728, and repaired the ship in Carlisle Bay, Barbados, after pounding through a few Atlantic storms. Sailing from Barbados to Virginia, he arrived in Hampton River, Virginia, on March 27, 1729, in need of more repairs, including a new bowsprit. Though his crew quickly replaced the bowsprit from a tree they cut six miles inland, Lingen waited in the Chesapeake until midsummer, when all the tobacco ships were ready to sail to London.[48]

Ludlow Castle sailed from Virginia on July 7, 1729, escorting the convoy of thirty merchantmen, including "*Princess Carolina*, Cpt. Halladay, 239 tons." Captain Lingen noted that the ships were top heavy: "They were very crank, part of their loading lying very high and having most or all their water stowed upon their decks." There must have been some problem, probably bad weather, for in two weeks they had not traveled far. On July 30 the convoy was scattered by a severe storm approximately four hundred miles northeast of the Chesapeake. When the convoy reformed, two of the merchant ships were missing. Because the crew on another ship noted that pieces of a cabin, decorative stern carved wood, and many hogsheads of tobacco were floating on the sea, the remaining convoy presumed that both of the ships sank with all hands, and the convoy continued to London. *Princess Carolina* and *Francis* were the two missing ships.[49]

A consideration of all the evidence suggests that *Princess Carolina* survived long enough to sail into New York. A large wave may have hit the quarterdeck of *Princess Carolina* or *Francis* in the storm, taking off the carved work, the roof of the cabin, and possibly some of the crew. Possibly *Francis* broke apart and spilled out the tobacco casks. The *Princess Carolina* crew probably made any necessary repairs after the storm, possibly including a crude replacement of the foremast step, and sailed with whatever wind would take them generally west to the nearest good repair port, New York. Many transatlantic and coasting ships that became damaged in storms and collisions sailed into New York and other established colonial ports for repairs before continuing their journey.

In Manhattan, assessing severe damage, hogging (a common distortion of the hull), rot, shipworm damage, a contrary business situation, or a combination of these reasons could have caused *Princess Carolina's* owners to decide that the twelve-year-old ship was not worth repairing. Loading the cargo into a hired ship, buying another ship, or selling the cargo in New York to a London factor were all possibilities. New York records, including newspapers, are minimal and intermittent during the early 1700s, allowing these or other possibilities without a researcher finding any records in the archives. After the storm Halladay also disappeared from the available records. He may have been lost at sea in the storm, or may have retired from the sea after reaching New York, or may have continued in the business without leaving a trail in the records that still exist.

Before abandoning the ship in the harbor, the crew would have removed all its rigging and hardware since such things were especially expensive in the colonies. In all probability, new owners converted *Princess Carolina* to a floating warehouse, possibly with a retail section, using the hulk for approximately fifteen years to store New York exports awaiting shipment and imports in need of temporary protection. We have no evidence to support this except the remains on the hull of only about half of its outer sheathing and the common practice of eighteenth-century port operators. Merchants increasingly warehoused goods during the eighteenth century, but the buildings were relatively expensive to construct, and land adjacent to the quays was dear. Colonists, keen to use any resources available, typically did not leave an old ship unused as a derelict for long when it would serve well as a retail outlet or storage repository for their cargos.

CHAPTER EIGHT

Development of 175 Water Street, Manhattan

AID UP IN THE EAST RIVER, *Princess Carolina* witnessed rapid changes in the New York waterfront. As the city thrived throughout the early eighteenth century, port facilities needed to grow to meet the increasing demands of commerce. Larger ships could only touch the shore within the "stone dock" (basin), which was too small to service all the large ships. Many of the vessels still moored in the harbor and were serviced by lighters, flat-bottomed boats that could sail over the shallows to a quay or slip. In order to unload and load the ships efficiently, the New Yorkers needed to expand their harbor facilities out into deeper water. The Dutch had previously used wood, earth, and stone to elevate the low coastal land above the high water mark. By filling the intertidal and shallow subtidal areas of the shoreline to the street level, eighteenth-century British colonists could load and unload large trading vessels directly into and out of horse-drawn wagons, eliminating the extra steps of transferring cargo into lighters, moving the lighters, and transferring the cargo into ships and wagons.

Extending the shoreline was an organized affair using a water lot as the basic unit. The city government would issue a grant of each water lot, usually to the person whose land came to the shoreline at that lot. The water lot's width usually was the same as that of the owner's land lot, and it typically extended approximately 200 feet into the river. The agreement generally included the stipulation that the area be filled within a specified number of years and that a municipal street be included along the newly created shoreline or quay. Archaeological evidence indicates that the lot owners of each new city block usually cooperated to fill the water lots. Most often they cribbed the block with an interlocking structure of logs and filled the space with stone, soil, and refuse from the land and excess ballast from visiting ships. When an old ship was available, it might be incorporated into the new block as a substitute for other forms of cribbing the fill.[1]

The original high water Manhattan shoreline of the East River was built up by the Dutch to form Queen's Street, now Pearl Street. By 1730 the English had filled the intertidal zone out one block to the old low tide water line, from Pearl Street out to what became Water Street, for approximately two miles north from the Whitehall Battery at the southern tip of the island.[2] The new construction meant that water was always lapping against the new quays. At Burnets Key, between Wall and Crown streets, the colonists had already filled into the river another block to allow approximately twelve feet of water at high tide and eight feet of water at low tide. This was enough water to allow a crew to berth a transoceanic ship parallel to the quay at high tide and let it lie safely aground at low tide. Between the new blocks formed by the filling processes, slips were left to accommodate lighters and horse-drawn wagons at the various markets. Each slip evidently had its own specialty market, such as the Fish Market, Meat Market, Meal Market, and Fly Market (another meat market).

In 1813 seventy-six-year-old surveyor David Grim recorded the use of the New York slips in the mid-eighteenth century: "Those slips were formerly openings between two wharves, in the river, for horses and carts to enter, and there unload the wood boats; those boats would go into the slips at high water, and ground there, for the cartmen to enter from Pearl Street, in order to unload them."[3]

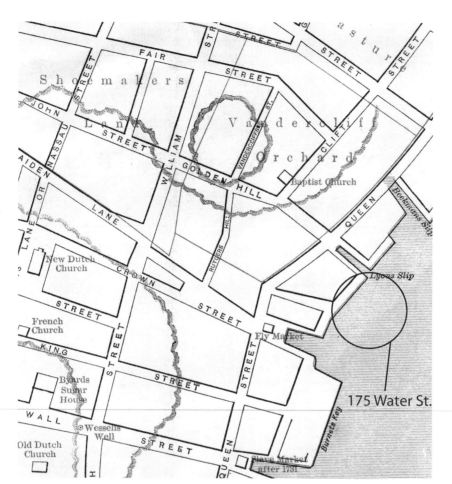

New York City and the East River in 1730, showing the location of 175 Water Street *Townsend MacCoun, 1909.*

With continued commercial growth the waterfront between Fletcher Street and Burling Slip (also "Lyons Slip," now John Street) quickly became a valuable piece of property in the 1730s. It was situated just up-river of the Fly Market and bordered the newly developing upper section of the port. A wharf area, which became Water Street, directly bordered the river at the low tide line. Along the west side of the street were commercial buildings on individual lots that faced the busy harbor. In the late 1730s the owners of those land lots applied for water lot grants for the east side of Water Street, across from their respective commercial buildings. That land was to become 175 Water Street.

A charter of 1731 gave the city council authority to grant water lots out to 400 feet beyond the low water mark. The nine grantees between Fletcher and John Streets were required to extend the width of Water Street to 45 feet, construct another 40-foot-wide wharf or street 200 feet out over the East River, and fill the area between Water Street and the new street for their own use within ten years. Evidently six of the lot owners, those of lots number one through six, coordinated

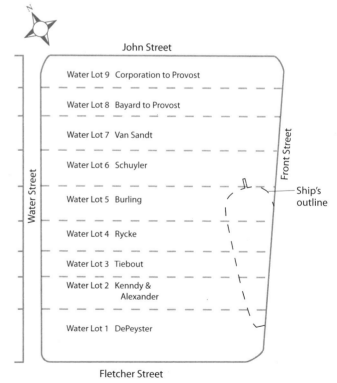

Site map of 175 Water Street with the water lots and grantees indicated. *Illustration by Warren Riess.*

their efforts to crib the fill for the deep end of their lots with an old merchant ship.[4]

All of the six water lots that eventually contained this ship were granted in 1737. Lot one belonged to Abraham De Peyster and his son Peter. Abraham De Peyster was a successful wine merchant and property investor who traded for decades with Madeira, London, and other owners of the block. Lot two was granted to James Alexander and Archibald Kennedy. Although little is recorded of Kennedy, except for his dealings through Alexander, records show that Alexander was a prominent citizen of New York. He was surveyor general of New Jersey, naval officer for New York, Kennedy's lawyer, part owner of a ship, and a merchant who traded with other colonies, London, and Lisbon. Lot three was granted to John Tiebout, a turner and part owner of the sloop *Mary and Margaret*. Henry Rycke, a blacksmith, received lot four, and Edward Burling, a merchant, was granted lot five. Lot six was granted to Elizabeth Schuyler, a widowed merchant who traded overseas and conducted a retail business in New York.[5]

From existing papers left by Alexander, De Peystor, and Schuyler, it appears that the lot owners conducted some business with each other over a long period of time. The three merchants used the same shipping agent in London, Rodrigo Pacheco. Pacheco, like Micajah Perry, conducted a complex business as shipping and buying agent, lender of credit, and ship investor. While the Perry firm consciously was not involved in any slave transactions, even though many of their clients were slave owners in Virginia and South Carolina, Pacheco and Alexander conducted a small amount of slave trading.[6]

Although these papers show the extent of the business dealings of the property owners, no archival record has been found of the methods used to fill the block, or the use of a ship as part of their filling process. The Alexander and Schuyler papers researched show no indication that these two merchants or their agent Pacheco conducted business with any of *Princess Carolina's* owners. One would imagine that Pacheco and Perry, both active shipping agents in London, would have conducted some business together, but perhaps it had nothing to do with the New York water lot owners. However, data obtained from the archaeological investigation of 175 Water Street, which included the Ronson ship site, and the investigation of other sites in Manhattan, provide much complementary information.[7]

The 175 Water Street block appears to have been

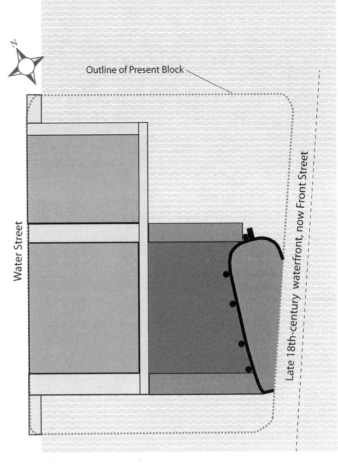

phase 1, cribbing
phase 2, fill in the western cribbing
phase 3, cribbing/pier, ship, and fill in the ship
phase 4, fill to the west of the ship
water areas left unfilled until later
● observed pile adjacent to the ship's hull

Early development of 175 Water Street, as indicated by archival and archaeological evidence. *Illustration by Warren Riess.*

filled in four processes that overlapped in time: (1) setting a crib for the western half of the block, (2) filling the western half, (3) cribbing the eastern half, and (4) filling the eastern half. Since the results of all four tasks show block-length rather than water lot–specific construction, it appears that the water lot owners cooperated closely to improve the block. The tasks can be dated by a combination of archival and artifact-related data.

In the first phase the colonists evidently set an interlocking framework of pine logs throughout the western half of the block sometime between 1737 and 1744. A 1735 map shows the area to be part of the East River, and the water lot grants were not given until 1737.[8] However, Grim's 1744 *A Plan of the City and Environs of New York* depicts the block as half filled.[9]

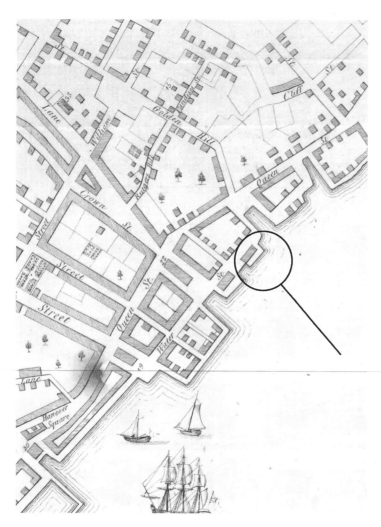

Map of Manhattan showing half of the 175 Water Street block filled. *A Plan of the City and Environs of New York as they were in the Years 1742–1743 and 1744* (New York: David Grimm, 1813). *Collection of the New York Public Library, image PSNYPL_MAP_304.*

similar cribbing construction north and south of 175 Water Street in the eighteenth century.[11]

The last dates of the artifacts indicate that phase two, the task of filling the western half of the block, was accomplished over a period of about forty years, between 1740 and 1795. The fill consisted mostly of earth, trash, and garbage originating on Manhattan. Some deposits of coral sand and cobble stone found in the fill appear to be excess ballast from incoming ships. The archaeological evidence indicates that the process took longer than originally suspected from observing eighteenth-century maps of Manhattan. Geismar reasoned that Grim's 1744 map depicted the western cribbing with the space only partially filled. She concluded that the buildings Grim showed on the site were built on piles over the partially filled cribbed space, as she discovered the remains of a six-by-seven-foot cribbed pillar in the western area.[12] The pillar may have supported one of the western buildings.

Phase three took place sometime between 1744 and 1755, when the eastern half of the block was cribbed with a combination of piers and a quay composed of

A 1757 view of 175 Water Street as part of the new waterfront. *A South East Prospect of the City of New York in 1756–7 with the French Prizes at Anchor* (unknown artist, c. 1757). *Collection of the New-York Historical Society, image 1904.1.*

It also shows that Water Street is fully constructed and widened, a row of buildings is constructed on the west side of the block, and a quay appears to be built out to approximately half of the final size of the lots. When excavating the site, Joan Geismar discovered that the framework consisted of a solid perimeter wall of squared pine logs, which were anchored in place by vertical piles and deadmen (attached horizontal logs). The deadmen extended perpendicularly to the walls, into the space to be filled. To keep the framework from floating, the builders placed field stones and gravel directly over the lower members of the cribbing.[10] Archaeologists investigating other Manhattan sites report wharfage and the old ship. Maerschalck's 1755 *A Plan of the City of New York from an Actual Survey* shows a completed block filled out to the eastern extent of the water lots, bordered at the East River with a new quay or street, and supporting the same buildings in the west that Grim showed. Except for the ship, and Deep Test No. 4 just west of the ship, none of the eastern half of the block was archaeologically excavated. All evidence for the colonial cribbing and filling of the eastern half comes from these two excavations and quick observations made after the archaeological work, when in two days the construction company removed the fill and cribbing with an excavator and bulldozer. Although the Maerschalck 1755 *Plan of the City* shows a squared-off eastern quay at the block, we were not able to see most of the crib material that made the eastern quay, except for the ship's hull.

Physical evidence around the ship indicates that two east-west solid wharves extended from the halfway cribbing to the final east wall. At the eastern end, the only part of the construction observed, the piers were made of log cribbing filled with rocks and earth. The bow of the ship was approximately two feet east of the eastern end of the northern pier. Next to the ship's knee of the head, two piles were driven into the mud, two-inch planks were spiked horizontally to the piles, and more spikes were driven through the planks and into the knee of the head. Similarly, the stern of the ship was spiked to planked piles approximately two feet from the southern pier's eastern end. The southern pier met the ship approximately five feet forward of the transom. We discovered no other means of fastening the ship to something stationary in the mud, though because of the nature of the excavation we may have missed them. Since the bow and stern spikes could offer only a light fastening for the ship, whoever placed the ship there must have intended that the ship be filled quickly to let gravity drive it into the mud and keep it in place.

During the excavation of the ship, we discovered that it had little of its original hardware aboard. Almost everything that could be carried or detached from the hull had been removed before the ship was filled with extraneous material. Only the lowest eight-inch layer of fill seems to have been part of the ship's ballast. Evidently the New Yorkers stripped the old merchant ship of its hardware and most of its ballast for salvage and to lighten the hull. They then floated the hull into a position parallel to the shore, spiked it to the horizontal planks mentioned, and filled it with excess ballast from other ships and soil and refuse from the city. The ship would have been at least partially filled before the block area just west of it was filled, since without the ship being stable in its position, the other fill would have slumped into the area occupied by the ship, pushing the ship aside.

We would have liked to discover the origin of the fill layers, but before we could send out the saved samples for analysis, someone in the laboratory ordered them thrown out "because they smelled." A loss, but not a major loss, because ships often unloaded excess ballast in a port's shallows, and other ships would pick up the "washed" ballast when they needed it. Thus, for example, on a Caribbean island a ship might pick up English flint ballast that another ship had previously dumped.

An analysis of the stratigraphy and types of material in the ship reveals clues to the filling process. The contents of the Ronson ship consisted of distinct layers of material that were not all level but were shaped to reveal the state of the ship's decks during the fill process. In the bow area, from the stem to the forward bulkhead, the space below the lower deck was filled with two distinct layers of material. The lower layer sloped down from the bulkhead, while the upper layer was relatively level. In the main cargo hold, between the two bulkheads, and below the lower deck, five layers formed two large humps—one under each of the ship's two cargo hatches. Aft of the after bulkhead, below the lower deck, the fill formed a fairly flat stratigraphy of two layers in a small space.

The shape of the stratigraphy indicated that the existence of the lower deck planks, when the ship was filled, was similar to the way we found it—the bow planks were intact, midship area deck planks were in position, and the aft planks had been removed. Therefore the workers filled the hull through the main and forward hatches in the cargo hold, while they dropped the fill between the deck beams in the aft section of the ship. The bow fill appears to be a combination of overflow from the forward cargo hatch fill and river silt from openings in the hull's bow. A consideration of each fill layer makes this interpretation clearer.

Layer 1, the lowest layer of fill in the ship, was a mixture of small tropical shells, coral sand, and silt. It lay relatively flat on the ceiling planks, averaging eight inches thick, and extended from aft of the forward bulkhead to at least the mainmast. The aft end of the layer was in a wall we could not excavate, and the layer

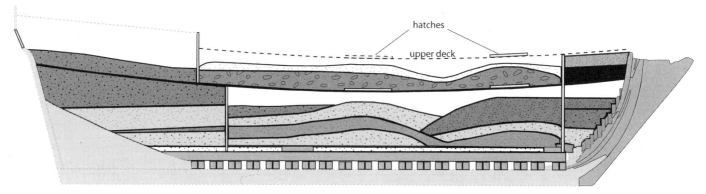

Side cutaway view showing the stratigraphy of fill found inside the ship's hull. *Illustration by Warren Riess.*

did not exist in the stern, where the distance between the lower deck and the ceiling planks was less than two feet. Artifacts found in layer 1 date to the first half of the eighteenth century, with a highest probability date in the 1720s.[13] The types of shells and coral indicated that it was not from a local source. Since this layer was flat and contained distinctly earlier artifacts than the other layers, while subsequent layers in the main cargo hold formed piles under the cargo hatches, there is a possibility that layer 1 was the remains of some of the Ronson ship's last sailing ballast. If that were so, the artifacts indicate that the ship stopped sailing sometime in the 1720s.

Layer 2 was the first fill we can be sure was added to the ship after it was placed in its resting spot. It consisted of coral sand and gravel below the main cargo hatch and in the after storage space. The layer formed a pile approximately two feet high directly under the hatch and one foot high in the after section and contained artifacts with a last date of 1744. Layer 2 probably was excess ballast on a ship entering New York's port in the 1740s. After unloading their cargo, the crew could have pulled the ship alongside the Ronson ship and unloaded her excess ballast through the vessel's main cargo hatch with baskets or pails.

Six more distinct layers of cobble, coral, coral sand, black volcanic sand, gravel, and silt filled the hull up to the lower deck. The latter material appears to be from the river bottom and may represent dredged material that accumulated in the man-made slips between the blocks. Men with shovels and mud tongs did such dredging in most eighteenth-century projects, though some larger European cities used horse-powered rotary digging devices. The eighteenth-century New Yorkers recorded the job of dredging the slips but did not mention how they accomplished it or where they dumped

the dredged silt.[14] The ship's hull would have been a handy receptacle for the dredgers.

Above the lower deck and below the nineteenth-century rubble, three distinct layers of fill existed. The largest was a layer that appeared to be fill from Manhattan, including pockets of earth, garbage, and commercial trash. In the midship area the upper deck was left in place and the space between decks was filled primarily with late eighteenth- and nineteenth-century land-based fill with large pockets of cobbles that may have been from the land or ballast from another ship. Above that and below the upper deck was a thick layer of white coral sand.

On the upper deck, forward of the mainmast were the remains of a small campfire, complete with stones and charred deck planks, indicating that the deck remained uncovered for at least a short time. From just aft of the mainmast to the stern the upper deck planks had been removed and the remaining upper space on the ship was filled with layer 11, composed of late eighteenth- and nineteenth-century land-based fill. Eventually the weight of the last fill and possibly subsequent building weight above the decks caused them to collapse in the bow and above the cargo hold.

Above the final layers were the basement floors of nineteenth-century buildings that had been constructed with brick and concrete and waterproofed with a 1-inch layer of asphalt below the basement floors. Outside the ship in the bow and stern areas, most of the material appeared to originate on land. Next to the bow was a small cache of broken fine pottery that may have been damaged in transit and discarded upon unpacking. Since time constraints precluded obtaining enough additional data about the fill between the ship and the halfway cribbing, the tale of the creation of 175 Water Street cannot be completed.

The lower stratigraphy within the ship was composed of ships' ballast, river silt, and gravel. Most of the upper stratigraphy came from shore, but whether it was moved to the site in the mid-eighteenth century or later is not clear. If the ship were completely filled by 1756 to satisfy the water lot grants, then possibly lighters moved the land refuse to the ship. The process would have included unloading wagons of fill into lighters at a slip, rowing the lighters to the ship's side, and then unloading the fill by carrying it over the sides of the ship. However, since a bulk wall existed approximately sixty feet to the west of the ship, and the ship and attached piles were a steady base, the construction of a sturdy pier to handle wagons may have been more efficient than using lighters. We found no archival or archaeological information to suggest which technique was used.

On the ship's upper deck a ring of stones around some charred decking, a small capstan, and the mizzen mast butt suggest that in the last half of the eighteenth century cargo handlers used the permanently bound ship as a new quay. A small fire would help keep them warm when working the waterfront in winter. The mizzen mast butt probably became the vertical mast of a cargo derrick, and the capstan, in the wrong position to be part of the ship's sailing furniture, likely served as its winch. These finds spark the imagination, and one can easily visualize the men standing near the campfire to keep warm on a winter day, waiting to unload a new cargo of British

goods into wagons pulled by teams of steaming horses waiting on the quay. Like people today, the workers probably wondered about the ship below their feet; or maybe they knew her story.

Eventually, progress-minded New Yorkers extended the land another two hundred feet to the east and raised it another eight feet with early nineteenth-century fill. Completely buried, the ship was forgotten as a small, unrecorded incident in Manhattan's history. During the nineteenth and early twentieth centuries the hull provided support for the merchant stores, warehouses, and apartments that occupied the block between Fletcher and John streets. This was a bustling area of New York's import merchant trade that was also close to the fish market area.

In the twentieth century downtown Manhattan grew vertically as technology allowed a more intensive use of every dear square foot of land. Tall office buildings bordered the block on three sides, and in 1960 the three-story nineteenth-century buildings on it were leveled to create a ground-level parking lot that remained active for twenty years. The HRO development corporation then applied to the city to construct a thirty-story office building that would cover the entire block, designated 175 Water Street. In one of the permits the New York City Landmarks Preservation Commission required HRO to conduct a preconstruction historical and archaeological investigation, and so Soil Systems hired Joan Geismar, whose team located the ship where it had been buried so long ago.

Postscript

AFTER THE SHIP WAS BURIED, the British Empire, including its American colonies, continued to expand and grow stronger. As the eighteenth century progressed, Charleston became less threatened as colonial and royal naval forces dispersed the pirates. British settlers colonized Georgia, thereby occupying former Yamasee territory and forming a new buffer against the Spanish in Florida. New York and Virginia, even in the face of repeated wars, continued to grow in population and economic vitality along with the entire British Empire.

The British Empire's trade accelerated, transatlantic shipping became less expensive, and ship design and construction progressed to incorporate scientific and engineering advances. By 1800 thirteen of the former American colonies had rebelled and became a separate, vibrant country—and still the remaining British Empire was the largest and strongest empire in history.

New York City grew only slowly until the nineteenth century, when it increased rapidly. In 1720 approximately 7,000 people lived in New York City, in 1850 it was home to approximately 500,000 people, and by 1980 there were 8,000,000 inhabitants plus tens of thousands who commuted every day into the commercial capital of the Western Hemisphere. New York has many superlative facets, especially its financial district, generally called Wall Street, which is the world's most powerful economic center. It was in the northeast corner of the financial district, after we completed the ship excavation, that HRO constructed the thirty-story office building that first housed the New York branch of the Westminster National Bank and is now owned by American International Group.

And what of *Princess Carolina*'s bow and artifact collection? At this writing in 2014, the Mariners' Museum in Newport News, Virginia, has preserved and housed the complete collection of timbers, artifacts, data, and photographs from the site. The collection includes 104 timbers, 179 planks, and 4 lead flashing strips, which together made up the first eighteen feet of the bow. They include the bow's fourteen-foot stem, frames, hull planking, and deck. The other approximately 2,000 artifacts are mostly ceramic and glass sherds, food bones, and other refuse from the land dwellers of New York. Only approximately 250 of the artifacts appear to be from between the ship's frames and the various layers of ships' ballast beneath the layers of landfill. The curated data at the Mariners' Museum include all the field notes from the excavation teams, the wood recording crew, and the hull recorders. Laboratory analysis and conservation records along with hundreds of detailed photographs and more than a thousand feet of high quality 16mm movie film of the excavation are also part of the collection.

This has been a thirty-two-year journey for me. Some of that time I was working only on the project, and at other times it was "stored in the freezer," but always it has been a bittersweet endeavor. My thirty-year-old daughter has never known a year when her father has not been trying to unravel the Ronson ship conundrum. When first told of colonial ship remains in New York, Sheli and I eagerly anticipated studying the site to answer historical and anthropological questions. While archaeologists had studied other ship remains in underwater and city waterfront landfill sites, none was an eighteenth-century British merchantman from the fleet that had been the red blood cells of the growing British Empire. I knew this vessel could offer some information and hoped it would be a relevant piece in the puzzle of the development of Manhattan from a small trading post to the world's greatest trading center. The ship turned out to be much more than that, compelling me through half a lifetime of research and analysis. Though frozen in place by fill, the ship was still able to take me, and I hope others, on journeys across the ocean and through time.

This multi-disciplined investigation has uncovered important information about the technology and industry of early Charleston, trade, and ships as well as small amounts of information about many aspects of American colonial life and the developing British Empire. People of eighteenth-century New York, Charleston, Virginia, London, and even Barcelona, Lisbon, and Madeira have become an integral part of the study because though they were thousands of miles apart, they were connected by *Princess Carolina.*

That I was eventually able to answer some of the questions about eighteenth-century transatlantic ships, and ask a few more, has been gratifying. I have not completed this task and will continue to research archives to discern even more. Pushed to the limits during fieldwork and then facing long gaps in subsequent research, we made mistakes; although these were mostly neutralized later, I have included them in this account to show the reality of rescue archaeology and what can go wrong. To write this book when some of the research project is unfinished may seem presumptuous, yet to wait until all studies of possible sources are exhausted would delay it for years with no guarantee of significant results.

Piecing the study together from distant and different types of information humbles me in the hope that the threads with which I bind historical and archaeological information together are not too thin. I apologize to those individuals who designed, built, sailed, and buried the ship if I have misinterpreted what they left behind.

I hope that the excavation, study, and remains of this ship continue to bring awareness and some understanding to many people of the significance in world history of the shipbuilders, merchants, traders, and mariners of the colonial Atlantic world. For people interested in maritime history and archaeology, the ship's remains provided many more technical questions and answers than I can present in this volume. As I finish this book, I have started a second wherein I will address more technical aspects of the ship's design and construction and will include many detailed illustrations of its remains.

NOTES

CHAPTER 1

1. Fredrik Henrik af Chapman, *Architectura Navalis Mercatoria* (Stockholm, 1768; New York: Praeger, 1968).

CHAPTER 2

1. Robert Grumet, *The Lenapes* (New York: Chelsea House, 1989); Robert S. Grumet, "The Minisink Settlements: Native American Identity and Society in the Munsee Heartland, 1650–1778," in *The People of Minisink*, ed. D. G. Orr and D. V. Campana (Philadelphia: National Park Service, 1991), 211–38.

2. Anne-Marie Cantwell and Diana diZerega Wall, *Unearthing Gotham: The Archaeology of New York City* (New Haven: Yale University Press, 2001), 78–84.

3. Oliver A. Rink, *Holland on the Hudson: An Economic and Social History of Dutch New York* (Ithaca: Cornell University Press, 1989).

4. Cantwell and Wall, *Unearthing Gotham*, 78–84.

5. William R. Shepherd, *The Story of New Amsterdam* (New York: Holland Society of New York, 1917), 85–86.

6. Robert G. Albion, *The Rise of New York Port (1815–1860)* (New York: Charles Scribner's Sons, 1939), 2–3, 80–81.

7. As quoted in Bayrd Still, *Mirror for Gotham* (New York: New York University Press, 1956), 17.

8. New York Naval Office Shipping Lists, 1715–1749, British National Archives, Colonial Office records, CO 5.

9. Albion, *New York Port*, 2–6.

10. William Burgis, "A View of New York, c. 1717, from Brooklyn Heights," in Issac N. Stokes, *The Iconography of Manhattan Island, 1498–1909* (New York: Robert H. Dodd, 1915), plate 25.

11. Details of the development are presented in chapter 8.

CHAPTER 5

1. Thomas Oertling, *Ship's Bilge Pumps: A History of Their Development, 1500–1900* (College Station: Texas A&M Press, 1996)—an excellent presentation of available material about such ship pumps.

2. Jay Paul Rosloff, "The Water Street Ship: Preliminary Analysis of an Eighteenth-Century Merchant Ship's Bow," master's thesis, Texas A&M University, 1986.

3. Arthur P. Middleton, *Tobacco Coast: A Maritime History of Chesapeake Bay in the Colonial Era* (Charlottesville: University of Virginia Press, 1953), 108, 123.

4. Ralph Davis, *The Rise of the English Shipping Industry in the 17th and 18th Centuries* (Newton Abbot, U.K.: David and Charles, 1972), 286–88.

5. Davis, *English Shipping*, 71.

6. Chapman, *Architectura Navalis*, 83–84.

7. House of Commons Journals 1745–50, 761–765—as cited in Davis, *English Shipping*, 74.

8. William Sutherland, *The Shipwright's Assistant, or Marine Architecture*, 2nd ed. (London: Mount, Bell, and Smith, 1726), 35; J. Richard Steffy and Peter Throckmorton, personal communication, 1987.

9. J. Richard Steffy, personal communication, 1987.

10. Howard Chapelle, *The History of American Sailing Ships* (New York: Bonanza Books, 1935), 67; Mungo Murray, *A Treatise on Ship-Building and Navigation* (London, 1754), 154; Sutherland, *Shipwright's Assistant*, 66–67, 75.

11. Edmund Bushnell, *The Complete Ship-Wright* (London: George Hurlock, 1669); Brian Lavery, ed., *Deane's Doctrine of Naval Architecture, 1670* (Greenwich: Conway Maritime Press, 1981); Sutherland, *Shipwright's Assistant*; Murray, *Treatise on Ship-Building*; Chapman, *Architectura Navalis*.

1. Brian Lavery, ed., *Deane's Doctrine of Naval Architecture, 1670,* (Greenwich: Conway Maritime Press, 1981).

2. Sutherland, *Shipwright's Assistant,* 87.

3. John J. McCusker, "Colonial Tonnage Measurement: Five Philadelphia Merchant Ships as a Sample," *Journal of Economic History,* 27 (1967): 82–91; Gary M. Walton, "Colonial Tonnage Measurements: A Comment," *Journal of Economic History,* 27 (1967): 392–97; Christopher J. French, "Eighteenth-Century Shipping Tonnage Measurements," *Journal of Economic History,* 33 (1973): 434–43.

4. Albert Sebille, *Histoire de la Marine* (Paris: L'Illustration, 1934), 195; Chapman, *Architectura Navalis,* plates I–XXV.

5. Chapman, *Achitectura Navalis.*

6. Fredrik Henrik af Chapman, "The Chapman Collection" (MS, available on microfilm), Swedish Maritime Museum, Stockholm.

7. David R. MacGregor, *Merchant Sailing Ships 1775–1815: Their Design and Construction* (Watford, U.K.: Argus Press, 1980), 20–24.

8. Chapman, *Architectura Navalis,* 86.

9. William A. Baker, *The Development of Wooden Ship Construction: A Brief Historical Survey to the Nineteenth Century* (Quincy, Mass.: N. A. Hamlin, 1955), 28, 30.

10. Chapman, *Achitectura Navalis,* 5–7; Chapman, "The Chapman Collection."

11. Chapman, *Achitectura Navalis* plates LII and LIII; MacGregor, *Merchant Sailing Ships,* 21–23.

12. Brian Lavery, *The 74-Gun Ship Bellona* (London: Conway Maritime Press, 1985), 10; Peter Marsden, *The Wreck of the Amsterdam* (New York: Stein and Day, 1975), plate XII.

13. Sebille, *Histoire de la Marine,* 146, 196; Jean Boudriot, *The Seventy-Four Gun Ship: A Practical Treatise on the Architecture,* trans. David Roberts (Beccles, U.K.: William Clowes, 1986), plate XV.

14. Carl Olof Cederlund, in discussion with the author, 1986.

15. Rosloff, "Water Street Ship," 71; Lester Ross, *Archaeological Metrology: English, French, American, and Canadian Systems of Weights and Measures for North American Historical Archaeology* (Ottawa: Parks Canada, 1983), 77.

16. Christopher J. French, "The Longevity of Ships in Colonial Trade: Some Further Evidence," *International Journal of Maritime History* 3, no. 1 (1991): 159.

17. Joan Geismar, ed. *The Archaeological Investigation of the 175 Water Street Block, New York City* 2 vols. (Marietta, Ga.: Soil Systems, 1983), 2: 698.

18. Geismar, *175 Water Street,* 2: 698; Ivor Noël Hume, *A Guide to Artifacts of Colonial America* (New York: Alfred A. Knopf, 1976), 298–303.

19. W. M. Harlow and Ellwood S. Harrar, *Textbook of Dendrology,* 3d ed. (New York: Sterling Publishing, 1950), 372–73; Virginia Steele Wood, *Live Oaking: Southern Timber for Tall Ships* (Boston: Northeastern University Press, 1981), 8.

20. Wood, *Live Oaking,* 8, 15, 46.

21. Harlow and Harrar, *Dendrology,* 85–95.

22. Harlow and Harrar, *Dendrology,* 230–35.

23. Wood, *Live Oaking,* 15.

24. Ruth D. Turner, *A Survey and Illustrated Catalogue of the Teredinidae* (Cambridge, Mass.: Harvard University Press, 1966), 6–8.

25. Turner, *Teredinidae,* 93, 111, 258–61.

26. Ruth D. Turner, in discussion with the author, April 1983.

27. Amy Friedlander, "175 Water Street History," unpublished report (Marietta, Georgia: Soil Systems, 1981); Alexander Papers, manuscript, New-York Historical Society; Account Book of Ann Elizabeth Schuyler, 1737–1769, manuscript, New-York Historical Society.

28. David Grim, *A Plan of the City and Environs of New York in 1742–44* (1813), and F. Maerschalck, *A Plan of the City of New York from an Actual Survey in 1754* (1755), both in Stokes, *Iconography of Manhattan,* plates 32a and 34.

29. New York Naval Office Shipping Lists (hereafter cited as NOSL), British National Archives (hereafter cited as BNA), CO 5 1222–1226.

30. *New York Gazette and Weekly Post Boy,* January 2, 1732 to December 1759.

31. Joseph A. Goldenberg, *Shipbuilding in Colonial America* (Charlottesville: University Press of Virginia, 1976), 53; Davis, *English Shipping,* 67.

32. Converse Clowse, "Shipowning and Shipbuilding in Colonial South Carolina: An Overview," *American Neptune,* 44 (1984): 229.

33. New York NOSL, BNA CO 5/1224; Virginia NOSL, BNA CO 5/1443.

34. Admiralty Passes, BNA Adm. 2357.

35. Cpt. Lingen to Lords of the Admiralty (August 27, 1729), BNA Adm. 1/2038.

CHAPTER 7

1. Hypothetical conversation based on circumstantial evidence provided later in this chapter.

2. South Carolina NOSL, BNA CO 5/508; Gov. Robert Johnson to Lords for Trade and Plantations, November 9, 1734, *Records in the British Public Record Office Relating to South Carolina* (Columbia: South Carolina Department of Archives and History, 1928–47), 36 vols., 18: 174–93 (hereafter cited as *Records in the BPRO South Carolina*); Lords Proprietors of South Carolina to the Governor's Officers, et al., February 23, 1716, *Records in the BPRO South Carolina*, 6: 148; Clowse, "Shipowning and Shipbuilding in Colonial South Carolina," 227.

3. Converse Clowse, *Economic Beginnings in Colonial South Carolina 1670–1730* (Columbia: University of South Carolina Press, 1971). Most of the general information in this chapter about South Carolina's early economy is from this source.

4. James F. Shepherd and Gary M. Walton, *Shipping, Maritime Trade and the Economic Development of Colonial North America* (Cambridge: Cambridge University Press, 1972), 73–90.

5. Shepherd and Walton., Shipping, 60, 157–61.

6. *Records in the BPRO South Carolina*, vols. 6–9.

7. Gov. Robert Johnson to Lords of Trade (November 9, 1734), *Records in the BPRO South Carolina*, 18: 174–93.

8. South Carolina NOSL, BNA CO 5/508.

9. *Collections of the South Carolina Historical Society*, vol. 5 (1897), 434; *South Carolina Historical Magazine* 33 (1932): 298; 9 (1908): 142; 21 (1920): 139–43.

10. Wragg Family Papers, South Carolina Historical Society, Charleston.

11. Steven Taylor, "Princess Caroline of Brandenburg-Ansbach," *Oxford Dictionary of National Biographies* online, http://www.oxforddnb.com/index/101004720/.

12. *Records in the BPRO South Carolina*, 7: 71.

13. South Carolina NOSL, BNA CO 5/508.

14. Robert W. Stevens, *The Stowage of Ships and Their Cargoes, Freights, and Charter Parties* (Plymouth: Stevens, 1859), 193.

15. R. James Ringer and Michel J. Audy, "Cargo Lading and Ballasting on the 16th Century Basque Whaling Vessel *San Juan* (1565)," *Proceedings of the 13th Conference on Underwater Archaeology*, San Marino, Calif., 1984, 20–22.

16. Clowse, *Economic Beginnings*, 133–34.

17. Stevens, *Stowage*, 192, 275; Ringer and Audy, "Cargo Lading," 24–26.

18. Stevens, *Stowage*, 275.

19. Clowse, *Economic Beginnings*, 122–33.

20. This and the next paragraph on rice stowage are from Stevens, *Stowage*, 193–95.

21. South Carolina NOSL, BNA CO 5/508.

22. Clowse, *Economic Beginnings*, 133–34.

23. Clowse, *Economic Beginnings*, 209, 175, 169.

24. South Carolina NOSL, BNA CO 5/508.

25. South Carolina NOSL, BNA CO 5/508.

26. New York NOSL, BNA CO 5/1224; Virginia NOSL, BNA CO 5/1442.

27. Jacob Price, *Perry of London: A Family and a Firm on the Seaborne Frontier, 1615–1753* (Cambridge, Mass.: Harvard University Press, 1992).

28. Seaman's Sixpence, BNA Adm 68/194 f.84.

29. New York NOSL, BNA CO 5/1224.

30. *South Carolina Gazette*, December 2, 1732, 3.

31. New York NOSL, BNA CO/1224.

32. Virginia NOSL, BNA CO 5/1442.

33. Felipe F. Armesto, *Barcelona: A Thousand Years of the City's Past* (New York: Oxford University Press, 1992), 37, 39–40.

34. Virginia NOSL, BNA CO 5/1442.

35. Armesto, *Barcelona*, 81.

36. Middleton, *Tobacco Coast*.

37. Price, *Perry of London*, 36–69.

38. Virginia NOSL, BNA CO 5/1442.

39. Middleton, *Tobacco Coast*, 212.

40. Middleton, *Tobacco Coast*, 254, 355; Virginia NOSL, BNA CO 5/1441–5/1444.

41. Middleton, *Tobacco Coast*, 113, and chapter 4, reference note 33.

42. Seamens' Sixpence Ledgers, BNA Adm 68/194, f. 131.

43. Virginia NOSL, BNA CO 5/1442.

44. David Hancock, "Self-Organized Complexity and the Emergence of an Atlantic Market Economy, 1651–1815: The Case of Madeira," in *The Atlantic Economy during the Seventeenth and Eighteenth Centuries*, ed. Peter A. Coclanis (Columbia: University of South Carolina Press, 2005), 30–33.

45. Alfândega do Funchal, liv. lu6 jl.uov.

46. Virginia NOSL, BNA CO 5/1442.

47. Virginia NOSL, CO 5/1443; Seamen's Sixpence Ledgers, Adm. 68/194 f. 182; Alfândega do Funchal, liv. lu6 jl.uov.

48. David Lyon, *The Sailing Navy List: All the Ships of the Royal Navy–Built, Purchased and Captured, 1688–1860* (London: Conway, 1993), 47; Cpt. Lingen to Lords of the Admiralty, BNA Adm. 1/2038, January 10, 1728–29,

undated 1728–29, March 24, 1728–29, April 21, 1729, May 21, 1729.

49. Cpt. Lingen to Lords of the Admiralty, BNA Adm. 1/2038, August 27, 1729; *New England Weekly Journal* 136 (October 27, 1729): 2.

CHAPTER 8

1. Norman Brouwer, "The Ship in Our Cellar," *Seaport* 14, no. 3 (1980): 20–23; Amy Friedlander, "Historical Research," in *The Archaeological Investigation of the 175 Water Street Block, New York City*, ed. Joan Geismar, 2 vols. (Marietta, Georgia: Soil Systems, 1983), 1:32; Andrea Heintzelman, "Colonial Wharf Construction: Uncovering the Untold Past," *The Log of Mystic Seaport* 37, no. 4 (Winter 1986): 124–35, reference note.

2. Stokes, *Iconography of Manhattan*, 243.

3. Quoted in Stokes, *Iconography of Manhattan*, 271.

4. Friedlander, "Historical Research," 25–30.

5. Friedlander, "Historical Research," 23–29.

6. Alexander Papers, Journal and boxes 1–3, New-York Historical Society.

7. Rodrigo Pacheco, "Alexander Papers (1737–1746)," New York Historical Society, box 6; Account Book of Ann Elizabeth Schuyler, 1737–1769, New-York Historical Society.

8. "Plan of the City of New York in the Year 1735," in Stokes, *Iconography of Manhattan*, plate 30.

9. Grim, *A Plan of the City*, in Stokes, *Iconography of Manhattan*, plate 32a.

10. Geismar, *175 Water Street Block*, 2: 689.

11. Geismar, *175 Water Street*, 2: 689.

12. Geismar, *175 Water Street*, 2: 692–93.

13. Geismar, *175 Water Street*, 2: 697–98.

14. Geismar, *175 Water Street*, 2: 679.

GLOSSARY OF SHIP AND
ARCHAEOLOGY TERMS USED

Adze. Woodworking tool with its blade attached perpendicular to the axis of the handle, used by shipwrights to shape and smooth timbers.

Aft. Toward the back or stern of a ship.

Amidships. The point on a vessel halfway between the stem and stern.

Apron. A curved internal timber, attached to the lower end of the stem and the forward end of the keel.

Athwartships. Across the longitudinal axis of a ship.

Ballast. Heavy material such as iron, stone, or sand placed in a vessel's hold to lower the center of gravity and increase stability.

Baseline. A graduated line, often a long measuring tape, secured on both ends to be the datum or reference line for an archaeological excavation.

Beak. A ship's forward protrusion at the bow; see Knee of the head, as it is technically called.

Bark. A general term often used to designate a small ship with three masts, a small warship, or sometimes a three-masted ship without a mizzen top-sail.

Beam. (1) A transverse timber that supports a deck and holds the sides of a ship together; (2) the width of a ship; see Breadth.

Bevel. See Chamfer.

Bilge. The curved portion of a hull beneath the waterline.

Bitts. Upright posts for belaying ropes or anchor cables.

Bluff bowed. Having a rounded rather than a sharp bow entrance.

Bolt. Cylindrical metal fastener used to fasten a ship's timbers or the chainplates of the standing rigging or for securing tackle, cables, and standing rigging; a variety of types exist: clench bolt, drift bolt, eye-bolt, forelock bolt, and ring bolt.

Bow. The forward end of a ship.

Bowsprit. A spar that angles forward of the bow and serves to extend the head sails and to secure the stays of the foremast.

Breadth. The width of a ship; molded breadth is the width at the outside faces of the frames; extreme breadth is the width to the outside of the planking.

Breast hook. A horizontally oriented knee fitted inside the bow to fasten the stem, apron, and forwardmost frames together and reinforce the entire assembly.

Bulkhead. An upright partition within a hull.

Bulwarks. Frame ends and planking that extend above the edge of a ship's uppermost deck.

Butt. The end of a plank or timber that is cut perpendicular to the length of the piece.

Butt joint. The meeting of two ship timbers or planks with their ends cut perpendicularly to their lengths.

Cant frames. The frames at each end of a hull that are not perpendicular to the keel. Those at the stem slant forward; those at the stern slant aft.

Capstan. A vertically mounted winch drum of heavy wooden construction used to lift anchors or other heavy objects. Sometimes called a capstern in ship contracts.

Carling. Short stiffening timbers located between and perpendicular to deck beams.

Caulking. Filling materials such as oakum, cotton fiber, and tar, driven or poured onto a ship's plank seams, to render the hull and decks watertight.

Ceiling, or ceiling planks. The internal planking of a ship.

Cheek. A horizontal reinforcing knee between the side of the bow and the knee of the head.

Chine. The angular join between the bottom and side of a vessel, typically found on flat-bottomed boats.

Chock. A wedge of wood secured across the butt of two frame timbers.

Clamps. Thick internal strakes, generally opposite wales, that reinforce the sides of a vessel. See Strake, Shelf clamp.

Coaming. The raised border around a hatch designed to keep water out.

Cockett. An official document listing cargo for which custom fees have been paid.

Collier. A ship used to transport bulk cargo, especially coal.

Companionway. Stairs between decks, or small deck openings designed for crew access between decks.

Compass timber. Naturally curved timber used for frames, stems, or other hull elements.

Crib, or cribbing. Interlaced logs or other material used to contain fill, such as rocks and soil, in submerged areas along the shore, for bridge supports, etc.

Cutwater. The forwardmost part of the stem that forms a curved leading edge, widest at the top. The cutwater is designed to part the water as the vessel advances.

Deadwood. Longitudinally oriented reinforcing timbers bolted to the top of the keel.

Deck beam. An athwartship timber that supports a deck.

Depth of hold. The centerline distance between the top of the floor timbers and the top of the deck beams at the midship frame.

Double framing. A term used to describe frames composed of two rows of timbers.

Draft. (1) The depth of water a ship draws; (2) a two-dimensional delineation or plan that shows a ship's design or construction features.

Draft marks. Lines or numerals carved into or attached to a ship's stem and sternpost to indicate how deeply the vessel is sitting in the water.

Drift bolt, or drift pin. A metal bolt driven into a hole of slightly smaller diameter.

Dunnage. Brushwood, scrap wood, or other loose material laid in the hold to protect the cargo from water damage or prevent it from shifting, or to protect the ceiling from abrasion.

Entrance. The foremost portion of a hull below the waterline.

Entrepôt. A port or other trading node, typically servicing a hinterland, where merchants store and distribute, import and export goods.

Factor. An employee sent to another port to conduct business there on behalf of the firm.

Fair, or fairing. To correct discrepancies in a ship's drawing.

False keel. A timber fastened to the bottom of the keel to protect it from damage or increase the vessel's draft. Also called a shoe in some ship contracts.

Fashion piece. A frame that defines the shape of a vessel's stern.

Firring, or furring. An outer layer of disposable soft wood, nailed outside the hull's outer planking, to absorb damage from shipworms and small accidents; also called sheathing.

Floor. The timber of a frame that is fastened across the keel; also called a floor timber. Also, the area above the floor timbers and their related ceiling planks.

Flyboat, flute, etc. A large, beamy, relatively flat-bottomed ship meant to be efficient by having a high cargo to crew ratio.

Fore-and-aft rig. A sailing rig with the sails set parallel to the axis of the keel. Common fore-and-aft rigs during the early eighteenth century include sloops and schooners; fore-and-aft sails of this era include gaff, stay, jib, and lateen sails.

Forecastle. The part of a vessel forward of the foremast; also a raised deck at the bow of a ship.

Foremast. The foremost mast on a ship-, brig-, or schooner-rigged vessel.

Forward. Toward the front or bow of a ship.

Foot wale. A thick longitudinal ceiling plank located at the floor head line or turn of the bilge.

Frame. The skeletal structure of a vessel mounted perpendicularly to the keel and composed of a floor timber and several futtocks. Sometimes informally referred to as a rib.

Futtocks. The upper timbers of a frame.

Garboard. The external planking strake that is closest to the keel; typically its inboard edge is shaped to fit into a groove or rabbet carved into the top of the keel.

Gripe. (1) A curved stem element that extends from the forward end of the keel up to the knee of the head; (2) the tendency of a vessel to point its bow into the wind when sailing close-hauled.

Gunport. A square or rectangular opening in a ship's side for a cannon.

Gunwale. The uppermost wale or strake on a vessel's side.

Half frame. A frame that does not extend across a keel but instead rises up from either side.

Hanging knee. A vertically oriented, angled reinforcing

timber, mostly used to strengthen the join between deck beams and the side of the hull.

Hatch. An opening through the deck of a ship.

Hawse pieces. Internal bow timbers that abut the frames and run parallel to the stem.

Hawse pipe. An opening at the bow of a vessel, often fitted with a sleeve of lead or other metal, through which an anchor cable passes. Also called a hawse hole.

Heel. (1) The lower end of a frame timber, end post, mast, or bowsprit; (2) the leaning of a vessel to one side due to the pressure of wind on the sails, unbalanced loading, or taking in water.

Hog. The tendency for a vessel's ends to droop due to the lack of longitudinal strength, overloading of the ends, or excessive strain in heavy seas.

Hogshead. A wooden cask that varied in size, but held approximately 64 gallons in the eighteenth-century British Empire.

Hold. The interior space in the bottom of a vessel that contains cargo or supplies.

Keel. The backbone of a ship, to which the stem, sternpost, and frames are attached.

Keelson. An internal longitudinal timber, set atop the frames directly over the keel, that serves to reinforce the hull longitudinally.

Knee. An angled timber used to reinforce critical joins in the hull.

Knee of the head. An inverted knee fastened to the forward face of the stem, designed to serve as a cutwater and to support the headrails and ship's figurehead.

Knightheads. (1) The forwardmost frame timbers in a ship's hull that are fitted parallel to and on either side of the stem; their heads can rise above the deck to form bitts that support the bowsprit; (2) bitt posts used to secure anchor cables or a ship's running rigging.

Lateen. A fore-and-aft rig common to Mediterranean ships (and widely used on mizzen masts of ships) with a large triangular sail spread by a long yard hanging diagonally from a short mast.

Lateral drift. The tendency of a vessel to move sideways as it advances through the water, generally caused by a combination of winds, waves, and currents.

Ledge. A small athwartship beam located between larger deck beams.

Lighter. A small boat, often flat bottomed, used to load and unload larger vessels that are at anchor.

Limber boards. Ceiling planks immediately adjacent to the keelson, generally left unfastened to permit access to the bilges.

Lodging knee. A horizontally oriented, angled reinforcing timber, generally fitted between deck beams to strengthen the join between the beams and the side of a hull.

Logwood. (*Haematoxylum campehianum*) A species of wood from Central America, the heartwood of which supplied a valuable dye in the colonial period.

Lower deck. On this ship what also might be called the *main deck*, just above the waterline and running from the stern to the bow in one sweep.

Main hatch. The largest hatch leading to the central cargo hold, often found just before the mainmast.

Mainmast. The tallest mast on a vessel, usually the central mast on a ship-rigged vessel and the second mast on a brig- or schooner-rigged vessel.

Margin plank. See Nibbing.

Mast. A vertically oriented timber or assembly of timbers, typically made of pine or similar light, strong softwoods, used to support a vessel's spars and sails.

Mast partners. Fore-and-aft beams or carlings that support a mast where it passes through a deck; also called mast carlings.

Mast step. A mortise cut to fit the heel of a mast; the mortise may be cut directly into the keelson or be in a block of wood fastened atop the keelson.

Midships. The center of the ship, either fore-and-aft or port-and-starboard.

Midship frame. The widest frame on a vessel.

Mizzen mast. The third mast on a ship-rigged vessel.

Molded dimension. The measurement of a timber from the inside to the outside of a vessel.

Mold frame. A frame that is designed and then constructed and placed on the keel to conform to the original ship design.

Monkey pole. A stanchion with notches in it for climbing into and out of the hold.

Mortise. A recess cut into the surface of one timber to fit the heel or tenon of another timber.

Nibbing. The squaring of deck plank ends where they meet the side of the hull, intended to reduce the likelihood of splitting. A nibbing strake, or margin plank, extends along the inside of a vessel's waterways and is notched on its inboard edge to fit the nibbed ends of the deck planks.

Oakum. Caulking composed of old hemp rope fibers soaked in pitch or tar and driven into planking seams to render them watertight.

Orlop. The lowest possible deck, just above the keelson or deadwood of a ship.

Outboard. Located toward the outside or completely outside of a vessel.

Outer planking, or just planking. The outer surface of a ship's hull.

Partners. Reinforcing timbers set around a deck opening to support deck features such as masts or bitts.

Planking strake. A continuous line of planks from stem to stern.

Port. The left-hand side of a vessel, when one is facing forward. Also referred to as larboard.

Privateer. A privately owned and operated warship that was licensed to conduct warfare against a country's enemy during times of war until the early nineteenth century.

Pump well. An opening between or on top of frames where bilge water collects and where a pump for removing the water is located; pump wells are typically found near the base of the mainmast.

Rabbet. A groove cut into each side of the keel, stem, and stern, into which the garboards or plank ends are seated.

Rake. The angle at which the stem slants forward and sternpost slants aft; also used to refer to the aft-slanting angle of a mast.

Riding bitts. Heavy upright posts to which anchor cables are secured.

Rudder. The blade hung on a vessel's sternpost by metal hinges that pivots to one side or the other to control the direction of a ship.

Sawyer. A skilled workman who, usually with an apprentice, shaped a ship's planks and timber with large handsaws.

Scantlings. The principal framing timbers of a vessel, or the dimensions of those timbers.

Scarf. The joint connecting two timbers.

Scow. A flat-bottomed boat with blunt or square bow and stern.

Scupper. A water drain on a vessel's deck.

Scuttle. (1) A small opening for light and air in the deck or side of a ship; (2) to sink a ship intentionally.

Seam. The longitudinal joint between two timbers or planks.

Sheathing. A thin layer of disposable soft wood, nailed outside the hull's planking, to absorb damage from shipworms and small accidents; also called firring or furring.

Shelf clamp. A clamp timber that also supports deck beams along its upper edge.

Ship. Generally, any large seagoing or lake-going vessel; specifically, a three-masted, square-rigged vessel.

Shipwright. A builder of ships.

Shipworm. Any of a number of species of mollusk that enters a ship's wood and tunnels through it.

Shoe. See False keel.

Sloop. A fore-and-aft-rigged vessel with a single mast.

Spars. The long wooden elements of a sailing rig used to spread the sails.

Square frame. A frame that is perpendicular to the keel and extends across both sides of the hull. See Frame.

Square rig. A sailing rig with the sails set perpendicular to the axis of the keel. Common early eighteenth-century square rigs included the ship and the brig.

Stanchion. An upright supporting post.

Starboard. The right-hand side of a vessel when one is facing forward.

Station lines. Geometric lines drawn on the plan of a ship's hull to illustrate its transverse shape.

Stem. The upward-curving timber attached to the forward end of the keel.

Stern. The back of a ship.

Stern knee. An angled timber that reinforces the join between the keel, stern deadwood, and sternpost.

Sternpost. An upward-angling timber attached to the after end of the keel.

Strake. A continuous line of planks extending from the stem to the stern.

Sweep. A large oar, worked by crewmen standing inboard of the bulwarks or rail, who push or pull on the sweep.

Tenon. A projecting element on a timber that fits into a corresponding mortise on another.

Tonnage. The carrying capacity of a merchant ship, by volume rather than by weight.

Trunnel. A wooden dowel (originally called a treenail) driven into a hole drilled to the same or slightly smaller diameter; used to fasten hull timbers, usually external planking to frames.

Turn of the bilge. The area of a hull where the bottom curves toward the side.

Waist. The part of a ship's upper deck located between the forecastle and the quarterdeck.

Wale. A thick planking strake that reinforces the side of a vessel.

Watch. (1) The division of time and duty aboard a ship, typically measured in four-hour intervals; (2) the division of the crew for alternating watch periods.

Waterline. The horizontal line on a hull that represents the water level on the outside of the ship when it is fully loaded.

Waterway. A strake or timber located at the juncture of the deck and bulwark; on some vessels this timber was hollowed to channel water to the scuppers.

Weather deck. The uppermost and thus uncovered deck.

Well. See Pump well.

Whelps. Vertical features that extend outward on a capstan to catch a line wrapped on them.

Windlass. A horizontally mounted winch drum fitted to upright posts, used to lift anchors or other heavy objects.

Yard. A spar of pine or similar softwood that tapers at either end; suspended from a ship's mast, the yard spreads the head of a square sail.

Colorado College Library
Colorado Springs, Colorado